W0037960

PLAY BALL

Lessons Learned on the Diamond

"Tim Boese on the Little League mound at Artesian Park in Lake Bluff, Illinois where his career began."

TIM BOESE
ILLUSTRATED BY TERRY DEMALINE

Copyright © 2019 by Tim Boese

All rights reserved. This book or any portion thereof may not be reproduced or used in any manner whatsoever without the express written permission of the publisher except for the use of brief quotations in a book review.

Print ISBN: 978-1-54395-662-7

eBook ISBN: 978-1-54395-663-4

DEDICATED TO HAROLD BOESE AKA BOESIE OR HAL–FATHER, HUSBAND, GRANDFATHER, TEACHER, AND MY BASEBALL COACH

"Selling Christmas Trees with my father in 1959...I'm in front"

"With Dad in Venice, Florida 2006"

FIRST INNING

I LOVE SPORTS. NOW MY WIFE, SUSAN, WOULD TAKE this to another level by saying that sports are my life, but that would be a bit of an exaggeration. Clearly, family, friends, and faith are at the top of my priority list, but I'll have to say sports solidly makes it to the top five.

I've participated in sports as far back as I can remember. In my early years, the 1950's through the 1970's, it was primarily centered on team sports like football, basketball, and baseball, with minor dabbling in individual sports like tennis and golf. As I got older, individual sports became a more prominent part of my physical activity. The fact is that I love to compete, whether it is in a team sport with my teammates or just challenging myself to get better at something that might be as simple as how many shots it takes to clear off the entire pool table. Fortunately, I was blessed with a reasonable level of dexterity, hand-eye coordination, muscle memory, and the ability to achieve some level of success. As the old adage goes, "I'm jack of all trades and a master of none." Then again, the beauty of any sport is that you can always get better; the journey never ends.

Having stated my love for sports in general, my motivation for writing this book focuses on one sport in particular—baseball. Baseball was not only the one sport where I've had the most success over an extended period of time, but also the sport I am most passionate about to this day. It's for this reason that I wanted to share my passion and document my personal history and thoughts on America's favorite pastime.

I've learned a lot of lessons playing baseball that have served me well in life, in business and in my personal relationships. Baseball in many ways is a timeless sport, and perhaps some of my stories and experiences will strike a nostalgic chord with others.

Passion can play a very important role in your life, whether it is collecting art, wine, playing bridge, painting, or gardening. It is always a pleasure to interact with people who have a similar passion to yours so you can compare your thoughts, build friendships around your mutual interest, and help each other expand their knowledge through your relationship. Passion for something can significantly enhance the quality of your life. It literally can "keep you off the streets" and propel your life down a positive avenue. If every child in this country developed a passion for a hobby, a sport, or a social cause, our country would be more civilized and prosperous.

My hope is that this book will allow those who are passionate about baseball to relive some of their own personal moments and memories with the sport. Whenever I talk baseball with someone, they always ask, "Well what position did you play?" When I tell them I was a pitcher, they say, "Oh, so you can throw but can't hit?" Actually, later in my career that would be right.

Early on in life, it became very apparent I had the ability to pitch, flip, or throw things and hit the target.

In Lake Bluff, Illinois, where I grew up, we had an annual Fourth of July celebration. It was a very typical small town event with a parade, carnival, fireworks, and a sock hop for the kids in the evening. The local residents ran the event, and all the proceeds went to the village to fund park renovations, village beautification, and support village services. It was small town Americana at its finest, with a parade featuring the Garden Club sponsored Lawnmower Brigade, local businessmen marching in formation with their briefcases, and the police and fire fighter equipment on display. The kids had their bikes decorated, and every local politician was waving at the crowd from a vintage convertible.

At the carnival, the local villagers staffed and ran the booths and games. My favorite was a ring toss game, where you had to throw a small wooden ring over long colorful canes hanging in a mesh rack about eight feet away. Now in the center of the array of canes was one with a dollar bill attached. I was only nine or ten at the time and barely able to reach over the barrier that distanced you from the canes. Each player was given six rings for a quarter to try to toss over a cane. Well, after I was ringing that dollar cane at the rate of at least two out of six, and even when the people running the booth would bunch more canes around the dollar cane in hopes of stifling my success, I kept on ringing the money cane. When I had pocketed about $25 and showed no sign of losing my touch, the local villager running the booth, a friend of my father, called him over and said, "If you don't get Timmy out of here, we aren't going to make any money for the village this year." With a little smile on his face, my father took my hand and marched me out of the carnival. A pitching career began.

Just like a baseball game, this book has nine innings. Each inning covers an era in my baseball career, whether it's hardball or later in life with softball. After each inning I've tried to capture the life lessons that I learned during my time on the diamond. I hope that somewhere in this nine-inning game of my life, I will put a little smile on your face or maybe cause a little chuckle as you reflect on your own baseball experiences. This book project has also allowed me to reconnect with old friends and teammates who have shared their thoughts, memories, and perspective on the sport. These are captured in "On the Roster" profiles in chapters two through eight, along with my personal "scouting report" on each individual. Their comments and input have helped to keep me honest, factual, and humble about my baseball career.

As a former great baseball player once said, "The older I am, the better I was." How true that is about so many things in life. Each inning also includes what I call a "Bullpen Session," which takes a deeper dive into some aspect of the game. Finally, each chapter concludes with a quote from one of the many famous and incredible personalities that have made baseball such an endearing sport for so many Americans. So with that—its time to "Play Ball."

Bullpen Session

Team sports vs. Individual sports

When I started my sporting life in the 1950's, it pretty much centered on team sports like Little League baseball, park district youth football, and grade-school basketball. While individual sports like tennis and golf were available, they just weren't on my radar. I think it is very important for kids to participate in both team sports and individual sports because there are different dynamics and lessons to be learned from each.

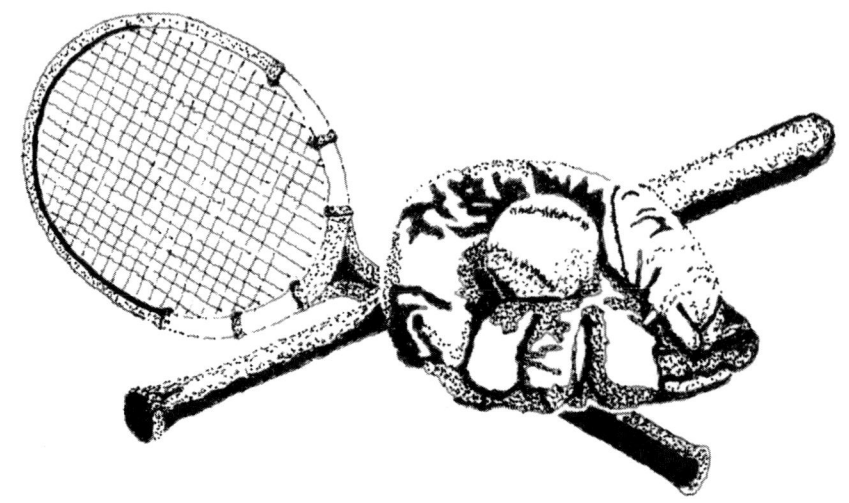

With team sports, you learn collaboration, mutual trust, leadership, and how to support your teammates. With individual sports, there is a tremendous emphasis on self discipline, dedication, and maintaining a positive attitude when things don't go as planned.

When you're a part of a team sport, you win together and lose together. If you make an error in a critical spot, commit a stupid penalty, or miss the key shot as the buzzer sounds, you feel like you've not only failed yourself but the entire team. Your role as a member of the team needs to be one of support and compassion for your teammates.

When you lose in an individual sport, the burden is on you to determine how you can correct your mistakes and hopefully perform better in the next competition. You have to be your own primary support mechanism.

I also think it's important for kids to participate in a variety of sports to find the one where their skill set fits best as opposed to specializing year round in one sport, which is much more common today. I loved going from one sports season to another, a different group of guys, a different conditioning process, and a different dynamic and challenge for your mind and body. As you get older, team sports often fall into the rear view mirror. They can become more physically demanding and require a higher dedication to conditioning in order stay competitive, and quite frankly it's hard to get nine old men together to take the field. If you want to continue to compete, there is always golf, bowling, or you can take up playing Texas Hold 'Em. I know one thing for sure, a couple beers with the boys after any sporting competition is one of the great joys in life, so if you can, then you must "Play On."

Baseball Quote

"To me, baseball has always been a reflection of life.
Like life, it adjusts, it survives everything."

- Casey Stengel

Second Inning

}}

AND SO MY STORY BEGINS. SLOWLY AT FIRST, BECAUSE in the 1950's in Lake Bluff we didn't have tee ball or coaches pitch like they do today. Organized baseball didn't begin until you were nine years old and eligible to play Little League. But with my older brother Tom to nurture me along my journey, my love of the game began at a very early age. I will say Tom introduced me to the game in an auspicious way. He was taking a few practice swings and unfortunately my head got in the way. I was only about four or five at the time, but my first encounter with a Hillerich & Bradsby bat is still evident with a scar running through my left eyebrow. Needless to say, this may have dented my head, but it didn't dampen my enthusiasm for the game.

Probably one of the greatest moments in anyone's baseball career is getting their first "real" glove. Not one of those cheesy little plastic ones that you probably put on the wrong hand and ran around with everyone saying "Oh look at little Timmy, isn't that cute." What I am talking about is a brand new leather glove like a Rawlings or Wilson model with a big league name etched in the leather.

In those days, Maurice Bluhm, my grandfather and a diehard Chicago Cubs Fan, used to take us to a game at the friendly confines of Wrigley Field. He lived in Winnetka, Illinois, up the lakefront north of Chicago. Typically if you live north of the Chicago River you are a Cubs fan, and if you live south of the river you are a White Sox fan. Ernie Banks "Mr. Cub," was the Cub's star shortstop. He never played for another Major League team, was a 2-time National League MVP, a 14 time All Star, a member of the All Century team and was inducted into the Hall of Fame in 1977. It was a thrill to go see Ernie play. He was famous for saying on a sunny day "Let's play two." Every year, for some reason, we targeted a game when the Cubs played the Philadelphia Phillies.

I will never forget walking out the tunnel at Wrigley Field and my first view of a Big League baseball diamond. I've never seen anything so green and so perfectly manicured. During that era, the Phillies center-fielder was Richie Ashburn. Richie, a future Hall of Famer and six time All Star and National League Batting Champ, was a very exciting player to watch. He even spent a couple years with the Cubs. My first real baseball glove was a Richie Ashburn model, something I will never forget. No wonder he was one of my first baseball idols. You always remember the name in your first glove, like the first girl you kissed, and that would be Daphne Knoll.

In the early years before I was old enough to play Little League, I was able to play in the Lake Bluff summer camp baseball program. Every weekday morning from nine to eleven at Artesian Park, the Park District conducted a baseball camp for all the local kids. Whitey Olsen and Dick

Watson were the men who ran the program; they were probably in college at the time. I would jump on my bike each day, hang my glove on the handlebars, and I would go to the park—it was pure joy. At the end of the summer, they always had an outing to a Cubs or White Sox game. You'd pack a lunch, they'd rent a school bus, you'd put on your cap, and of course you'd take your glove for the foul ball you were sure to catch. It was an end of summer ritual and it was always exciting to go to a Big League ballpark.

Probably the most beneficial factor for my baseball development was my older brother Tom. I can't overstate the value of having an older brother to help you develop your baseball skills. Not only was Tom always willing to play catch or throw each other grounders, but I was able to play with his older buddies, which really helped me "up" my game. Fortunately, I was able to compete with them at a young age and not just get stuck in right field to fill a spot. My dad was my coach from Little League all the way through American Legion baseball, when I was 18. There is no question in my mind that a strong father-son relationship is also a huge factor in the development of future baseball players.

The movie "Field of Dreams," one of my all time favorites, probably captures the essence of the father/son relationship better than I can possibly capture in this book. If you are passionate about the game and your father has been involved in your baseball career, then it is impossible for you not to be emotional or even shed a tear when in the closing scene Ray Kinsella, played by Kevin Costner, is reunited with his father John to play a little catch. It is magical.

Contrary to my grandfather's love for the Cubs, my father was a New York Yankee fan and therefore favored the American League Chicago White Sox over the Cubs.

As a result, my favorite team of all time has to be the 1959 "Go Go" White Sox. I remember riding back from Iowa, after our summer ending trip to my father's family farm in Iowa (or is it heaven), listening to the radio when the White Sox clinched the pennant over the Cleveland Indians to go to the 1959 World Series. Unfortunately, they lost to the Los Angeles Dodgers four games to two. The team was filled with great personalities like Little Louis Aparicio, Nellie Fox, Ted Kluzewski, and Early Wynn.

I can remember going to a White Sox game and sitting in the upper deck down the left field line. One of my favorite players on the team was Orestes "Minnie" Minoso. Minnie was the first black player on the "pale hose." He hit a homerun on the first pitch he faced as a White Sox. While Ernie Banks was "Mr. Cub", Minnie Minoso was "Mr. White Sox." Unfortunately, Minnie Minoso had been traded to Cleveland in 1957 for Early Wynn, but came back to the White Sox in December of 1959 and Bill Veeck awarded him an honorary pennant championship ring. He was a right hand hitter with a very open stance. Every time he came up, my father would say, "Now be ready, because with that open stance, he might just hit a foul ball right to you." I was poised and ready with my Richie Ashburn glove even though we were sitting probably 600 ft. from home plate. I mean…if you can't trust your father.

With dad as the coach and Tom playing Little League, any summer travel plans had to wait until after the season ended. Usually this would involve a trip to my father's childhood farm in Linn Grove, Iowa or a fishing trip to Wisconsin or Minnesota. Our gloves, balls, and a couple bats, and of course my sister Beth, always made the trip. In those days, there wasn't an abundance of drive-in restaurants, let alone fast food, so invariably my mom packed lunch and we'd look for a roadside park and picnic table. These stops always involved playing catch before we got back on the road to our destination. Baseball was in my blood. All I needed now was to make it to nine years old and I'd get a uniform and be on a real Little League team.

Lesson Learned

EVEN THOUGH I WAS A LITTLE BOY IN THE PRE-LITTLE League phase, there are still important lessons to be learned. Developing a passion for a hobby or a sport at a young age is essential for achieving your maximum potential. Working on the proper skills necessary for a sport at a young age programs your mind and body to its requirements. When you try to train yourself later in life, you probably have to break old habits. There is nothing better in life to keep you on a positive path than to be passionate about a sport or a hobby.

It's also important to keep a balance in your life with other priorities like academics and social interaction with your friends. We often hear of child prodigies who burn out because of pressure to succeed or perhaps their expectations exceeded their level of skill. These early years made me realize that excellence takes practice, dedication, and sacrifice. It helped me tremendously to be able to play baseball with my brother and his older friends. You get better faster out of necessity when you compete at a higher level of competition. Like many things in life, the harder you work, the luckier you get—baseball is no exception.

On the Roster

"Tom in Heisman Pose - DePauw University 1967"

Name - Tom Boese

Nickname - "Boesie" (Should be Junior)

Hometown - Lake Bluff, Illinois

Height – 6'1"

Weight - 175

Bats - Left, Throws - left

Position (s) - First base and outfield

Current Residence – Minneapolis, Minnesota

First Baseball Memory - Our mother, Betty, took Tim and me to see our father, Harold, play in a baseball game at Mooseheart, a boys home in the Fox River Valley, west of Chicago. We arrived at the game late and dad had already been taken to the infirmary after being spiked by a sliding base runner.

First Glove - Earl Torgeson Trapper Model

Favorite Team - Chicago White Sox

Favorite Player - Orestes "Minnie" Minoso - Chicago White Sox

Baseball History - Played Little League through freshman year baseball at DePauw University in Greencastle, Indiana.

Baseball Highlight - One of two sophomores on Lake Forest High School Varsity and reached base in first seven at bats on the Varsity team.

Best Baseball Memory - Heading into Comiskey Park for a White Sox vs. Yankees game and getting a big smile and hello from Jack Brickhouse, the legendary voice of the Cubs and White Sox. Also listening to Don Larsen's perfect game in the 1956 World Series in Mrs. Berry's fifth grade class.

Unique Baseball Experience - Going to a Cubs/Padres game in the afternoon at Wrigley Field and then going to the White Sox/Brewers game the same night at County Stadium in Milwaukee.

Remembering Tim- Yes, I hit him in the head with a baseball bat. It was clearly his fault walking into my swing path. One year I was home during spring break from college to attend a game at Grant High School when you pitched the first of five no hitters that spring and summer.

Work History - Liberal Arts College Administrator /Educator.

Biggest Influence - Father, Harold Boese

"Tom (center front) Lake Bluff Little League 1958"

Scouting Report

ALWAYS GREAT TO HAVE A BIG BROTHER WHO BLAZES the trail and helps you develop your skills. Tom is an easy going, fun loving, and excellent all- around athlete. He was probably a better hitter on the football field than the baseball diamond. Achieved Little All American status as a defensive safety at DePauw University and was inducted into their Sports Hall of Fame. Demonstrated what lack of fear and sheer determination can do for you on the gridiron. He was a natural teacher and mentor who allowed me to play with the older boys and accelerate my development. If you are drafting a trivial pursuit team, you will want to have Tom on your team. He knows more inconsequential facts and tidbits than anyone I know.

Bullpen Session

Taking Care of Your Glove

GETTING YOUR FIRST GLOVE IS A HIGHLIGHT OF A young baseball enthusiast's life. The smell of a new baseball glove is unforgettable. Taking care of your glove is a ritual. The first thing I did when I got that Richie Ashburn glove was apply the Neats Foot oil and leather conditioner. If you asked anyone today what Neats Foot oil is, I suspect they would scratch their head and send you to the closest podiatrist office. Actually it's made out of the feet and shinbones of cattle. Neat in the oil's name comes from an old English term for cattle.

Every night I pounded that glove with my fist and a ball to loosen up the glove and start forming the pocket, literally making it part of my hand. At night, I took a shoelace and tied a baseball into the pocket and actually slept with the glove. In fact, I never wanted anyone else to ever put their hand in my glove for fear that it might alter the fit for my hand (oops…the first superstition is entering the arena), more on that later.

I was also meticulous about making sure all the leather strapping was tied tight and in no danger of breaking. Many times over the years, I had to replace the strapping by connecting the fingers in the glove with new leather. A task that was not really very easy. Your glove is your baby and you need to treat it lovingly by protecting it and caring for it.

I remember once after a game I couldn't find my glove in the car and I was in a complete panic. Fortunately, I discovered that I had driven all the way home with the glove sitting on the roof of the car. What a relief. I wonder what happened to my Richie Ashburn glove; perhaps my mom threw it out with my baseball card collection. Oh well, that Honus Wagner card was never going to be worth much money. Over my entire career, close to sixty years, I have only had four gloves. My Denny McClain Model 31 that I got in 1968 is my third glove and it is still hanging in my garage.

Baseball Quote

"When I was a young boy I used to play baseball in my backyard,
or in the streets with my brother and the neighborhood kids.
We used broken bats and plastic golf balls
and played for hours and hours."
- Robin Yount

Third Inning

}}

THE MAGICAL DAY WAS FEBRUARY 4, 1958. I WAS finally nine years old and eligible to play in the Lake Bluff Little League. This was like a rite of passage—achieving manhood—or so it seemed that day. In Lake Bluff they had a draft of players, but if your father was a coach then you were automatically on his team. Having my father as my coach was wonderful. He was always available to play catch and encouraged me to stay the course when I would hit a bump in the road. If you survey all of the major league players today and asked who was the most influential person in their baseball career a very high percentage would say it's their father.

Now the Little League in Lake Bluff was divided into the minors and the majors with typically the nine and ten year olds filling the minor league rosters and the eleven and twelve-year olds the majors. While this was the norm, it was not the rule. Thanks largely to my competing with older brother Tom and his friends; I was one of three nine year olds to make the majors. At about a whopping 80 pounds and 5 feet, I could not be classified as a stud baseball player. However, one of the beauties of baseball is that size is not a limiting factor. Just think of some of the greats of all time like Peewee Reese, Little Luis Aparicio, and current players like the Boston Red Sox Dustin Pedroia and Jose Altuve of the Houston Astros. Baseball is an every man's sport and that's one of the reasons it is such an enduring passion for so many people.

One of the highlights of finally getting to play in an organized league was the uniforms. Fortunately due to the hard work of the Lake Bluff Little League Association and the support of the community we had a complete uniform—hat, jersey, pants, and socks. To a nine year old this was like being in the Big Leagues. Four teams were represented in the major league—Cubs, White Sox, Cardinals, and Braves. The uniforms had glossy logos of these teams stitched on—it was not some cheesy looking stencil job.

Opening day was a real happening in Lake Bluff because our volunteer fire department let the players ride the fire trucks around town before dropping the players off at Artesian Park for opening day. You can only imagine how excited this little baseball junkie was that day. While my records and memory of my initial couple of years are a bit sketchy, to the best of my knowledge, I competed well, pitched a little, but began to blossom when I hit my third and fourth years.

I must have also experienced losing in those first couple of years because I can remember sitting at the top of the stairs, in our house, crying my eyes out after one of those losses. Oh, the life lessons we learn when we are nine!

One of the controversies during these years was that the father of my best friend, Jeff Frees, also coached the team and as a result Jeff and I were always on the same team. This was tantamount to the "break up the Yankees cry" in the 1920's when the Babe Ruth led Yankees dominated Major League baseball. But we weathered the storm and Jeff and I stuck together throughout our Little League careers.

Playing for your father brought along additional responsibility because often times you were the de facto groundskeepers for the games. Although the Lake Bluff Park District maintained the diamonds, if inclement weather hit and threatened to postpone the game, we took off to rake and sand the field in the hopes that we would get to play.

Having your father there also meant you got some extra on the spot coaching and guidance. I remember in one game my father was coaching third when I was at bat and he gave me the "take sign," in other words don't swing at the next pitch. I either ignored it or perhaps missed the sign and proceeded to hit a homerun. After the game my father took me aside and asked if I had seen the take sign and I said "I did take the pitch, I took it right over the left field fence." He was pleased but not amused. Fathers can be very precise and literal, as we all know.

Another time while pitching I hit a kid in the head, by mistake of course. As he sat at the plate dazed and whimpering, his mom raced out of the stands and verbally assaulted my father saying, "Your kid throws too hard, he shouldn't be allowed to pitch in this league." My father, of course, said the pitch just slipped out of my hand.

As I said earlier, one of the wonderful things about Lake Bluff was that it was a very active and supportive community; a great place to grow up. The Little League was completely funded by the community through business donations and a fundraising activity of the annual Christmas Tree Sale. For a month before Christmas, in the vacant lot next to Bill's Dairy Market the Little League players and parents sold Christmas trees.

When I think of my father, perhaps he enjoyed nothing more than to sell those trees with his sons as his assistants. He was a natural born salesperson, a world-class schmoozer, and an artful BS-er. He commuted into

Chicago on the train for 40 years, and when the tree sale was on he took the early train home, slammed down dinner, and put on his selling shoes. I can still see him cutting the twine off a tree, stomping it into the ground to spread the branches. If there were a bad side to the tree, he'd just tell the prospective buyer to face that side into the corner of the room.

It was usually extremely cold during the sale and I enjoyed standing by the fire in the big metal trash barrel or sitting in the warming hut. But the bottom line is we raised a lot of money to have nice uniforms and a wonderfully run Little League. In fact when my father passed away in 2011, we designated the Lake Bluff Little League for donations in his honor.

All in all, my four years in Little League were glorious. Sadly, Lake Bluff was not affiliated with the National Little League Association and as a result we could not compete to qualify for the Little League World Series in Williamsport, PA. I'm sure we would have won. My final year statistics were solid, I lead the league in hitting at .484, tied for the home run lead, was 5-0 in pitching and my team, the Cubs, won the league at 10-2. My buddy Jeff Frees hit .333, with 3 homers, and a 4-0 pitching record-break up those Cubs—on to Pony League.

Lesson Learned

LITTLE LEAGUE WAS THE FIRST TIME THAT I PLAYED IN an organized league with umpires, official games, and had to follow the rules of baseball. I was a part of a team and had to learn how to interact with my teammates and opponents and how to handle my successes and failures. I had to listen to the coaches and understand that their comments and criticisms were meant to be constructive, to help you become a better player.

This was the first time that I had to learn how to encourage and support my teammates and how to win or lose with humility and dignity. You had to practice if you wanted to improve and make sacrifices to be part of the team. There may have been other things to do, but the highest priority was to be prepared for the next game, because your teammates depended on you.

On the Roster

"Brian in Vegas...Parred the hole just like Tiger"

Name: Brian Lofstrom

Nickname: Claims he never had one

Hometown: Lake Bluff, Illinois

Current Height: 6'2"

Weight: 180 pounds

Throws: Right

Bats: Right

Position Played: Infield

Current Residence: Las Vegas, Nevada

First Baseball Memory: Starting Little League in the minors in Lake Bluff, I hit a grand slam homer over the fence and that night I got a call from Mr. Ritter, our manager, that I was moving up to the majors

First Glove: Rawlings Luis Aparicio model

Favorite Team: 1959 Chicago White Sox

Favorite Player: Luis Aparicio - Chicago White Sox

Baseball History: Played Little League through 3 years of High School baseball

Remembering Tim: I was playing second base with a man on first when the ball was hit up the middle which I caught on the fly and tagged out the runner running from first base for a double play and helped preserve Tim's no- hitter.

Work Experience: Dentist for 38 years

Biggest Influence: My brother, Mike

"Lake Bluff Junior High Basketball".
(Brian back row third from left, Tim back row second from right)

Scouting Report

BRIAN IS AN OUTSTANDING ALL AROUND ATHLETE and a consummate team player. He played football, basketball, and baseball in High School. Brought up to the varsity basketball team as a sophomore, he was a deadly outside shooter. This is a guy you can depend on. He's trustworthy, honest and we have been friends for 60 years. He had very successful career as a dentist. He is always willing to give you a free examination. A golf fanatic who has relocated to Las Vegas, Nevada so he can play year-round.

On the Roster

"Grant in Dallas with wife Mary and a Dallas Cowboy Cheerleader"

Name: Grant Cardinal

Nickname: Carbodes

Hometown: Lake Bluff, Illinois

Current Height: 5'9"

Weight: 160

Bats: Right

Throws: Right

Positions played: Infielder

Current residence: McKinney, Texas

First baseball memory: Buying a pack of baseball cards for five cents and laying them out by position on the driveway and playing a make believe game. Also, riding my bike to the park with Jeff Frees and hitting grounders and fly balls to each other.

Favorite team: Chicago White Sox.

Favorite Player: Luis Aparicio - Chicago White Sox

Baseball History: Batting against Jay Hook in High School. He eventually played for the New York Mets. I hit .280 my senior year in High School

Baseball Memories: Reading the Sporting News cover to cover through High School, I was a baseball statistics junkie. When living in Austin, Texas I went to all the University of Texas baseball games to watch Burt Hooten and David Chalk play.

Unique Baseball Experience: I remember my sophomore year in High School playing a game in Antioch, Illinois. It was so cold I emptied all the bats out of the bat bag, and I climbed in and zipped it up to stay warm.

Memories of Tim: He was a feared Ace

Work History: Worked 23 years for Motorola Semiconductor in Austin, Texas

Biggest Influence: Father Earl who coached me in Little League

"Pony League Tim, Jeff Frees and Grant 1963"

Scouting Report

EVEN THOUGH GRANT GREW UP "ACROSS THE TRACKS" in Lake Bluff, his driveway was the place for pickup basketball games. He was a utility player on the baseball field and a quiet, lead by example kind of guy. Big time baseball statistics guy always good if you're into baseball trivia competitions. The skill set that he developed on the diamond has transitioned beautifully to the golf course and supports my belief that baseball players are the best all around athletes. Grant values his Lake Bluff roots and is always willing to make the extra effort to reunite with his L B buddies.

Bullpen Session

Street Games

WHAT A GREAT TIME IN LIFE; YOU ARE NOT A TEEN-
ager yet, and girls are just not that important. All you want to do is hangout
with your buddies and play baseball. The only problem was most times
you didn't have enough guys to field two full teams, so you had to impro-
vise. If you had just two guys you played catch or pepper, threw ground
balls to each other, or maybe even simulated pitching a game. If you had
three or four guys, you might play homerun derby or hotbox (you might
call it monkey in the middle). Now if you could get eight or ten guys, then
together you could play a modified game of sorts. You might have to close
right field thus anything hit there was an automatic out. You might play
pitchers hands where the batter is out if he doesn't reach first base, on a
ground ball, before the ball is thrown back to the pitcher. You may even

have "invisible runners" because you needed someone on base to bat. But you could still make it work. You just had to use a little ingenuity.

Growing up in Lake Bluff in the 50's and 60's there were a lot of vacant lots in the neighborhood where we could construct a baseball field and play our neighborhood games. You would use a piece of cardboard for the bases and your glove as home plate. Often the outfielders were in the street, and when a car was coming, a cry would go out indicating, "don't pitch." In those days most vacant lots and empty fields in America had a worn down configuration of base paths and a trampled down outfield. That's what kids did in the 50's and 60's. It was healthy and fun.

Having enough equipment—I mean bats and balls—was always a challenge. Invariably the bat might have a couple screws in it and electrical tape to stabilize a crack. There were no such thing as aluminum bats in those days and the balls might literally be beat into an oval or have a couple stitches snapped. Knocking the cover off the ball was a literal description of what happened sometimes.

Sadly when a house was built in the vacant lot, we had to look for another neighborhood field; but we always seemed to find a way to make it work. These were the days when our entertainment was outside all year round; just a group of kids being innovative, creating our own games and competitions. No video games, no Playstation, and no sitting inside gaming. We were exercising and interacting with our friends, and in my mind that's a simpler, healthier way to grow up.

Baseball Quote
"I didn't understand anything about playing baseball.
I started playing and it was enjoyable. Most of my life, I played with
older people on my team, in my league. I learned a lot about life.
Every day in my life, I learned something new from somebody."
- Ernie Banks

FOURTH INNING

GRADUATING FROM LITTLE LEAGUE TO PONY LEAGUE, age thirteen and fourteen, is a significant moment in your baseball career. Pony league is a transition, a bridge from Little League to "big boy" baseball. Not only are the kids getting bigger, stronger, faster, and more competitive, but because the dimensions of the field are growing. Instead of 60 ft. bases they go to 80 ft. and instead of a 46 ft. distance from the pitcher's rubber to home plate its 54 ft. The height of the pitcher's mound even grows to eight inches from six inches.

One big difference in Lake Bluff is we had fences in Little League, but not in Pony League so you had to run your butt off—maybe get lucky with a miscue by an outfielder—if you wanted to hit a homerun. Pony league was also the first time to compete against the surrounding towns like Lake Forest, Waukegan, and Libertyville. We got the opportunity to really see if we were competitive or just legends in our own mind.

Our pony league team was the Yankees, and once again, my father and Jeff Frees's dad were the coaches. The talent pool was narrowing a bit, but my buddies Jeff, Grant, Brian, and Kenny were the core of our success. Pony league was during middle school, so baseball was still limited to a summer activity. We won the league both years and in the league championship against Highland Park I pitched a five hitter and hit a grand slam to finish in a flurry and launch myself into my freshman year at Lake Forest High School, home of the Scouts.

Since Lake Bluff did not have a High School, we went to Lake Forest High School, and my enemies became my teammates. By now, at age 14, I was a brute of a man, a whopping 5'9 inches and 140 pounds. Playing baseball in the northern states in High School was always complicated by the weather. After basketball season ended in early March, baseball began and invariably, with snow still on the ground, you were playing catch in the gym. When you finally got outside, at best it was damp and cold. If you've ever taken batting practice in the cold with wooden bats, you know what it feels like when you hit one on the handle or the end of the bat. It feels like a thousand bee stings at once and your fingers feel hollow. But just as the mailman delivers the mail regardless of the weather, the game goes on.

In High School we had a freshman baseball team, a JV team, and the varsity. I got off to a fast start giving up just one hit in my first three games, two no hitters, and a one hitter. Brother Tom thought that was worthy of a submission to the "Faces in the Crowd" section in Sports Illustrated, but never got around to making a submission. I was now playing baseball essentially for six months out of the year. After freshman year I went right into summer Lake Bluff Colt League (ages 15 and 16). Like High School, this was now a major league sized field, 90 ft. bases, the pitching rubber was 60 ft. 6 inches from home plate and the mound was 10" high.

The players by now had a lot more body hair and had to wear a cup to protect the family jewels. I'm telling you all of this because as a pitcher a six month season for a 15 or 16 year old creates a lot of wear and tear on your arm.

With Colt League I was back to playing with my Lake Bluff buddies on the Pirates. I loved the uniforms, sleeveless for the first time with a big bad Pirate face logo. We were once again competing against the surrounding communities, including my former High School teammates in Lake Forest. Even though we were probably the smallest community in the summer Colt League, we were very competitive. We had epic battles with Waukegan, both years for the league title.

One memorable game occurred in Lake Bluff against Waukegan when, Ken Eiserman, one of our outfielders, and the Waukegan catcher, Joe Hall, had a huge collision at home plate. Kenny's mother was not happy with the Waukegan catcher who had violently applied the tag at home plate. After the game, behind the backstop, she let the Waukegan player know exactly how she felt, God bless her for standing up for her son. I can assure you Kenny did not need any help; he was on the football team in High School and college—he was as tough as they come.

Sophomore year in High School was a banner year in my pitching career. I started out pitching with the Junior Varsity team and was brought up to the varsity towards the end of the season. In my first game I threw a no-hitter against Grayslake. My sophomore year was the first time the Major League scouts began to appear at our games. In those days there were no radar guns, they simply used a stopwatch to time your fastball.

Later that summer, in my second year of Colt League, the press clipping would say I had two more no-hitters and a perfect game against Deerfield. Not sure if my memory is just failing me, but I doubt the perfect game. While I had good control, I can't remember a game where I didn't at least walk someone or hit a batter. But it is in print; there was no "fake news" in those days.

While baseball was clearly my best sport, I also played football and basketball for four years in High School. There are different skill sets for each of these sports. They require different conditioning regimens but the result of playing multiple sports is that it helps you develop versatility as an athlete. In today's world, kids specialize in one team sport with year round conditioning programs or simply play an individual sport. By doing this, I think they forego a lot of the benefits and discipline that playing multiple sports offers—benefits that can be valuable to them later in life.

When you're 17 or 18, your summer baseball is usually American Legion sponsored. My summer and High School career continued with a couple more no hitters and a Chicago Tribune all-star selection. But here is where the problem begins. While my passion for the game never wavered, unfortunately my shoulder decided it was overworked and just plain tired. Throwing a baseball creates tremendous stress on the body, shoulder, and elbow, and can be particularly damaging when you are still growing. A few cortisone shots kept me going, but clearly the damage was compounding. At this stage of my career, I basically had two pitches; throw it as hard as you can, and a curve ball I had thrown since Little League.

While I had a lot of arm trouble my senior year in High School, I still finished the year with 50 strikeouts in 35 innings and a 1.00 era. On 6/12/1967 I was drafted by the Cincinnati Reds and offered, as required, a minimum $350 a month salary to go to Wytheville of the Appalachian League. Their scout Dale McReynolds, who had been following me through my last three years of High School, was a fabulous person. He was very thoughtful and nurturing, providing tips on my pitching and generally excellent fatherly advice. He sent me multi-paged typed letters (that's with a type writer and white out for correcting typos) to educate me on the draft process and coaching recommendations.

That summer Dale took another draftee, Mike Mores, and me from the Chicago area to Sioux Falls, South Dakota, to work out with the Cincinnati Reds farm team. At the workout I got to watch their number one draft choice, (number eight overall in the draft), Wayne Simpson pitch. He was a 90+ mph pitcher with terrible control. In this game when he got it over the plate the opposition was hitting it 100mph the other direction. Eventually his control improved enough, and in 1970 he was brought up to the majors with Cincinnati and was a phenom for a couple years before his arm blew out. In the 70's there was no such thing as pitch count or Tommy John surgery, and Wayne's career was over early.

Having had no professional coaching as a pitcher, no one ever told me as a young growing boy that you should probably minimize the torque and wear on your arm caused by throwing a curveball. I should have stuck with just a fastball and maybe learned to change speeds and that would have gotten the job done. Until you are fully matured and you have finished your growth spurt, you should work on your mechanics and perfect your control. Just throw with a natural motion and don't torque your arm throwing curve balls or screwballs. Just think of the impeccable form of Nolan Ryan or the perfect control of Greg Maddux—all that it did was get them into the Hall of Fame, on the first ballot. I missed some starts my senior year in High School and spent some time with the Orthopedic doctors. Needless to say I turned down the professional offer and I decided it was onward to Miami University in Oxford, Ohio to continue my baseball journey.

Lesson Learned

AS I GREW OUT OF LITTLE LEAGUE AND INTO PONY and Colt league, the level of competition increased and my expectations of myself were elevated. The playing fields are bigger and the dimensions placed a greater demand on my skill set, athleticism, strength, and stamina. I was no longer playing and competing with boys I had grown up with; I was playing against teams in other towns and players that I didn't know. As a result, my sportsmanship was challenged. It was easy to be a sore loser and even a cocky winner at times. Suddenly I had to make my own decisions and judgments about new and challenging situations. It was important to develop some humility in order to handle myself properly whether I won or lost. I also began dealing with nagging injuries, arm fatigue, and soreness. It certainly isn't as much fun playing the sport that you love when you're in pain. You don't want to make excuses, but it is only natural that you want to perform at your optimum potential.

On the Roster

"Kenny 2018"

Name: Kenny Eiserman

Nick name: I-Z

Hometown: Lake Bluff, Illinois

Height: 5'10"

Weight: 170 pounds

Bats: Left

Throws: Left

Positions played: First base and outfield

Current Hometown: Libertyville, Illinois

First glove: Hand-me-down from brother Joel or Jerry

Favorite team: New York Yankees

Favorite player: Mickey Mantle-New York Yankees

Baseball History: Played Little League through High School baseball. All Northwest Suburban Conference in High School. Hit a homer in Little League off of Jeff Frees and later in the game struck out against Tim.

Unique Baseball Experience: Playing left field in High School, I tagged out a runner going to 3rd base.

Remembering Tim: It was easy playing the outfield in High School when Tim was pitching because no one hit the ball to me.

Work History: Started as a CPA in Lake Bluff and now have worked 30 years for a bank in Palatine, Illinois

Biggest Influence: My brothers, Joel and Jerry

Scouting Report

WHEN YOU GO TO WAR ON THE DIAMOND OR GRID-
iron, you want this guy by your side. He is a fighter, sheer determination
and guts are a part of his game. He is definitely not afraid to get dirty
on the football field or the baseball diamond. Comes from a long line of
top-notch Eiserman athletes. Loyal, trustworthy, and steady throughout his
life. Not fancy, no frills; just solid as a rock. I spent countless hours over at
the Eiserman house playing basketball in their back yard always followed
by an ice cold Coca Cola. Kenny's father, Jobie, was a local umpire and
referee and not a guy that you wanted to question with what you thought
was an improper call.

On the Roster

"Chuck at Lake Bluff Little League Field 2018"

Name: Chuck Johnson

Nickname: Chucky

Hometown: Lake Forest, Illinois

Height: 6'0'

Weight: 161

Bats: Right

Throws: Right

Positions played: Catcher and infield

Current residence: Lake Bluff, Illinois

First baseball memory: Waiting for dad to come home from work so we could play catch, field grounders, and I could pitch to him.

First glove: Wilson model

Favorite team: Modern day 2016 Chicago Cubs and 1959 Chicago White Sox

Favorite Player: Derek Jeter-New York Yankees

Baseball History: High School captain of the baseball team and all conference, selected to play on Waukegan colt championship team that lost to Gene Lamont Rockford team.

Baseball Memory: Just the joy of the game and being a good teammate.

Unique Experience: Was salesman for McGregor and Rawlings and as a result had access to Major League locker rooms.

Memories of Tim: Caught Tim's first varsity game when he was brought up as a sophomore and threw a no-hitter and helped us win the conference championship.

Current occupation: Investment broker for the last 30 years

Biggest Influence: My little league coach Tom Garrey. I also remember when I was a batboy for the Shoreline team and Tom was playing and our team was down by eight runs. He said that if we get a couple runs here and there we will win the game, and that's what we did. I will never forget that optimistic advice.

Scouting Report

A SOLID ATHLETE FROM A VERY ATHLETIC FAMILY.
Take charge guy from behind the plate who guided a young pitcher while making his first varsity start. Leadership skills translated well into successful military and business career. Chuck is one of those guys who hasn't changed over the years. He returned to his hometown to pursue his business career and continues to be a loyal supporter of local athletics. Go Scouts!

Bullpen Session

Collecting Baseball Cards

I'm thinking about starting a class action law-suit against Mothers who threw away their son's baseball card collection. I expect I would get thousands of participants. Sadly, these collections were just viewed as useless clutter with no sentimental or monetary value in the future. Thank God, I didn't own a Honus Wagner card or Mickey Mantle's 1952 rookie card. Like so many other kids in the 1950's you saved up your nickels and dimes to buy a package of Topps baseball cards. In the 50's, Topps literally had a monopoly on the industry. For a nickel you could get five or six cards in a pack and a flat piece of unusually hard bubble gum. For professional baseball players in those days getting your own baseball card was clearly an indication that you had made it, that you were in "The Show."

Almost all the cards I bought were from Mr. White's Variety Store in Lake Bluff. It was with tremendous excitement and anticipation that you would crack open the pack, stick the gum in your mouth, chew it until your jaw was sore, and see what cards you received. It was a crap-shoot for whose individual card you got, or perhaps you got a team photo. The cards had the player's picture or an action photo. On the back of the card were the player's career statistics, usually year-by-year, teams he played for, and vital statistics like hometown, height and weight, position, and whether he threw or batted right or left handed. You could purchase a file box for your cards but generally a shoebox with some cardboard dividers to separate the teams was the storage mechanism of choice. Then the swapping of cards began. First trying to eliminate your duplicates and then attempting to get the cards of your favorite players and teams. If you didn't trade the duplicates you could always clip them to your bike wheels and have them flap in the spokes. This made you bike sound like a motorcycle.

Your baseball card collection served as great entertainment for many rainy afternoons and perhaps helped develop your future business negotiation skills. I wonder if Theo Epstein of the 2016 World Champion Chicago Cubs honed his management skills as a child by collecting and trading baseball cards. But sadly you outgrew this stage of life, pushed the box of cards under your bed, or set them up on a shelf in your closet. Then the defendant in our lawsuit decided to clean out some unnecessary clutter and tossed them in the garbage with last night's table scraps. I would love to have my baseball card collection back.

Baseball Quote

"I think about baseball when I wake up in the morning.
I think about it all day, and I dream about it all night.
The only time I don't think about it is when I'm playing it."
- Carl Yastrzemski

FIFTH INNING

}}

COLLEGE BASEBALL DEFINITELY HAD ITS UPS AND downs, largely as a result of continued arm and shoulder issues. But I must say playing four years at a Division One school, graduating on time with a business degree and a Dean's List grade point average are accomplishments I am still proud of today. Even though the Cincinnati Reds drafted me right out of High School, I was not heavily recruited and while I was in contact with Miami University I actually walked onto the team.

Miami was going through a coaching change at the time with the retirement of Woody Wills, their long tenured coach of 40 years. Bud Middaugh, a Miami graduate, was taking over the program. I remember meeting with Woody during my senior year college visit; he was nice man, without a lot to say. But I was in love with the university and ready to take my chance with the baseball program. At the time I probably still believed that baseball could be my career.

Unfortunately 1967/1968 was the last year that freshmen were ineligible to play varsity baseball and as a result the freshman team played a limited schedule of about 20 games. Bud Middaugh recruited most of the freshmen and it was clear he was well on his way to building a highly competitive program at Miami. We had tryouts in the fall and I remember all the freshman pitchers lining up with a catcher in the outfield to show freshman Coach Rick Wessel our stuff. Now maybe my catcher just had delusions of grandeur, but after he had taken a few fastballs on his wrist, I think he just went back to the dorm to sign up for intramural football—too fast, too much movement. Our first freshman game was against Xavier and I got the nod to start. I pitched five innings and no batted ball got past the pitcher's mound—ten K's, no hits, a couple dribblers back to the mound, and a popup to the catcher and one to me. My first college appearance was in the book. Al Dukate, one of Bud's top recruits, from Lorain Admiral King in Ohio, pitched the last four innings and struck out eight guys and I'm not sure if they got a hit off of him. It was a great start to my college career. That year, the freshman team actually beat the varsity team in a full scale, all out practice game. Coach Wessel, who coached the freshmen, was elated, and while Coach Middaugh was upset, I think I detected a proud smile behind that scowl.

My arm held up for the limited freshman schedule and I was able to earn some scholarship money for the following year—a Walter "Smokey" Alston academic stipend. Walter was a Miami University graduate, a baseball and basketball player, and one of the greatest Major League baseball managers of all time. He was Manager of the Year six times, and inducted into the Baseball Hall of Fame in 1983. He was a lifelong supporter of Miami baseball and died in Oxford, Ohio in 1984. In fact, at an alumni game in Oxford in the early 1980's, "Smokey" was our manager and the great Joe Nuxhall, who pitched in the majors for 22 years, was our starting pitcher. My sophomore year, pitching on the varsity, was spotty at best with further arm problems (I will elaborate on that in the next chapter). I started mostly in non-conference games, pitched some relief, but most every night my arm was coated in Bengay and covered by a couple sweatshirts. This was probably not pleasant for my bunkmates at the fraternity house.

Pitching against Xavier that year, the team I pitched against in my first appearance at Miami, I found myself on first base, probably due to a walk. The first baseman asked what ever happened to those two guys we faced last year as freshmen. Sadly I had to say I was one of them.

Clearly my star was beginning to fade. I also didn't endear myself to coach Middaugh when on our spring trip I was wrestling with our star pitcher George Fannon in the hotel room and he cracked his head open on the bed post and had to miss his next start. He shouldn't have been picking on a rookie. In a letter that I wrote home that year I told my parents that I had met with Coach Middaugh and the team physician and we agreed that I should try and play outfield my junior year.

That experiment didn't work very well and it was emotionally challenging being on the team and not being able to contribute and earn my keep. My junior year was probably my low point in my baseball career, but I still loved being part of the team. By then, like most pitchers who aren't taking batting practice and the caliber of pitching has improved; I too had lost my hitting skills. When I didn't make the team for the spring trip my junior year, another teammate who suffered a similar fate, Chico Verelli, declared a road trip on our own to Florida. We had great time, but I would have rather been on the spring trip with my teammates.

I struggled through my junior year, lost my partial scholarship, and decided to take the summer off of baseball. Coach Middaugh and I also agreed I would skip fall baseball and try to come back in the spring at my own pace. Since Miami University did not have any "skin in the game," I asked Coach Middaugh, who happened to also be a fellow member of the Beta Theta Pi Fraternity, if I could play fraternity sports. So I played football and basketball my senior year with my Beta Brothers.

The comeback story, and a testimony to my persistence, occurred with my senior year. With rest and some rehab and a slow buildup to pitching again, I returned to the mound. My senior year I finished five and one with a 2.25 era highlighted by winning both ends of a double header against Bowling Green. I also earned Academic All Conference recognition. In the Bowling Green double header I was brought into the first game in relief and got the win. After the game, Coach Middaugh told me to just keep throwing in the bullpen because I was starting the second game. I pitched the first five innings, left with the lead, and got my second win of the day. All that pain and struggle was worth it.

We didn't win the conference title my senior year, losing once again to our archrival, the Ohio University Bobcats. The series against them created one of my most memorable, but sadly unsuccessful, highlights of my college career. The star of Ohio U was their future 1995 Hall of Fame shortstop, Mike Schmidt. Mike was, without question, the greatest college baseball player I had ever seen. His Major League career highlights included 548 home runs, 12 All Star games, 3 national league MVPs, 10 gold gloves, and a World Series Championship and Hall of Fame induction. Our rivalry with OU and in particular the competitive nature of the two coaches Bud Middaugh and OU's coach Bob Wren was beyond intense. I was brought into the game in relief and ultimately had to face Mike Schmidt. As he was stepping into the batter's box, Coach Middaugh stepped off the bench, walked towards the 3rd base line and said for all to hear, "knock him down." The next pitch was thrown a little inside, and Mike just ducked his head back a little bit, unfazed and no doubt unimpressed. Bud got up again and came to the mound to tell me that I better knock him down or I'll never pitch again. Coach Middaugh must have been chuckling inside because this was just about the last game of my college career. Since I take direction well and I'm highly coachable, the next pitch I threw over his head against the backstop. Thankfully he casually sat down at the plate—still very unimpressed. On the next pitch he smashed a hooking line drive down the 3rd base line, hitting in fair territory, scattering our bullpen and rolling off the end of the left field fence, into the parking lot for a ground rule double—my contribution to the legendary Hall of Fame career of Mike Schmidt.

Lesson Learned

COLLEGE BASEBALL CREATED AN ENTIRELY NEW CULtural challenge. I was away from home and having to manage all aspects of my life and integrate playing a sport with academics and having a social life. All of my teammates were essentially the stars of their High School teams and suddenly I was a little fish in a big pond. Added to this was my biggest challenge, my chronic arm issues that were affecting my ability to compete and perform. My sore arm became my constant companion, not only creating a physical challenge, but also a mental challenge to deal with the pain. It would have been easy to quit, but perseverance and tenacity kept me on the diamond—no pain no gain. It wasn't easy but probably because of my physical struggle it was more gratifying that I completed my four-year collegiate athletic journey. Learning to manage my time around academics and athletics continues to be one of my proudest accomplishments. I even got to provide a little "chin music" to Mike Schmidt.

On the Roster

"An All- American's swing-Denny Smith Miami University 1973"

Name: Dennis Smith

Nickname: Smittie

Hometown: Grew up on a farm near Weston, Ohio

Height: 6"4'

Weight: 210 pounds

Bat: Left

Throws: Right

Positions Played: First base and outfield

Current Residence: Bowling Green, Ohio

First baseball memory: Playing with older brothers in the barnyard. Used cow patties for bases, which didn't make my mom very happy. Modeled my swing after Dick McAuliffe and practiced by swinging a wooden handled scythe to chop soybeans and milkweed. Played imaginary games by throwing a rubber ball against the barn for grounders and up on the roof for fly balls.

First glove: McGregor first baseman glove that I still have.

Favorite team - Cleveland Indians

Favorite Players: Carl Yastrzemski-Boston Red Sox and Al Kaline-Detroit Tigers

Baseball Highlights: All Ohio at Bowling Green High School, First team all MAC 1971-1973, All American in 1973. Inducted into the Miami University Athletic Hall of Fame in 1990. Drafted 3 times eventually signing with the Texas Rangers

Best Baseball Memory: Winning Miami's first MAC championship in 1973 and going to NCAA tournament

Unique Baseball Experience: Playing right field when Miami played Toledo, I went back for a fly ball; fell over the snow fence and out of the ballpark. I knocked the ball back into the field of play and in an attempt to get back into the park, fell over the fence again. The runner completed an inside the park homerun.

Remembering Tim: Highest respect for you as a hard throwing no-nonsense pitcher who loved to compete and always gave us a chance to win. Proud to call you a teammate and a friend.

Work History: 30 years in public education with 10 years coaching baseball

---

Biggest influence: Oldest brother Dan taught me everything. Parents came to every college game in their pickup camper

---

Scouting Report

HE IS A BIG, POWERFUL OHIO FARM BOY WHO BECAME an all American at Miami University. Consummate teammate, highly coachable, dedicated to the sport, and a terrific guy to be around. Highly competitive on the field, wonderful role model who was willing to do whatever was necessary to produce a win—a true selfless player. Took tremendous pride in his accomplishments and continues to be very committed to Miami University baseball. He now loves to take his Motorcycle on cross-country trips and continues to hope the Cleveland Indians can end their 70 year World Series drought.

On the Roster

"Tim at Miami Baseball Field 2018"

Name: Tim Love

Nickname: Hoot

Hometown: North Olmsted, Ohio

Height: 5"11'

Weight: 175 pounds

Bats: Right

Throws: Right

Positions Played: Pitcher, first base, and outfield.

Current residence: Naples, Florida

First baseball memory: Going to Cleveland Indians game at Municipal Stadium versus New York Yankees in 1955 and seeing Mickey Mantle play.

First glove: Rawlings model Cal McLeish

Favorite team: Cleveland Indians

Favorite player: Bob Feller-Cleveland Indians

Baseball highlights: No hitter in Southwestern Conference 1967 summer league. Making freshman team at Miami University and being the winning pitcher with the game winning RBI versus the Varsity in a fall intersquad baseball game.

Best memory: Making the freshman team as a pitcher even though they had four pitchers drafted by the pros.

Unique Experience: After losing a close game, in an angry fit, I stomped on a batting helmet and had it stick to my foot as I got on the team bus in High School.

Memories of Tim: Having tryouts with Tim at Miami University, he was the fastest pitcher I had ever seen. Problem was that it was so straight that after three or four innings, they timed it and started to hit. Tim vigorously disagrees with this statement. But he does agree that he has lots of movement with his golf shots, unfortunately.

Work History: 42 years in advertising retiring as Vice Chairman of Omnicom group and CEO of Asia Pacific

Biggest Influence: My uncle Charlie

"Tim on the mound for North Olmstead 1967"

Scouting Report

HE HAS THE PERFECT BLEND OF ATHLETIC TALENT AND artistic flare. If your team needs a guy who can develop a plan, market the plan, and then execute the plan, then he's your guy. Had a plan to be a success in the advertising world, developed the skill set, marketed himself and achieved incredible success. Highly competitive with whatever he undertakes and is only limited by a set of "bad wheels." He is my inspiration for undertaking this book project. We were fraternity brothers and roommates in college and now neighbors and golf partners in Naples, Florida.

On the Roster

"Steve fishing in the Florida Keys 2017"

Name: Steven Rowe

Nickname: Boat

Hometown: Lima, Ohio

Height: 6'4"

Weight: 200 pounds

Bats: Right

Throws: Right

Positions played: First base and first base coach

Current Residence: Worthington, Ohio

First baseball memory: Putting on my Cleveland Indians uniform, which my grandfather gave me for my birthday. He convinced me that I would play centerfield for the Indians. He also taught me how to fish

First Baseball Glove: I have a picture on my desk taken 64 years ago when I was five years old with a three-fingered glove given to me by my grandfather.

Favorite team: Cleveland Indians

Player: Rocky Colavito- Cleveland Indians

Baseball History: League champs at Lima Senior and Ohio State Champions with Lima Blues American Legion team in 1967. Been an Assistant coach for 14 years with Thomas Worthington High School.

Best baseball memory: Son Pete hitting homeruns in High School and in college during his senior year on my birthday. My high school coach was a coach's Hall of Fame inductee—Joe Bowers nicknamed "Juice" because he would spray you with saliva when he "coached you up." His favorite saying was "Poke up and choke it,"—to spread out at the plate and choke up when you had two strikes. I used this philosophy throughout my coaching career.

Unique Baseball Experience: While I was coaching Worthington High School in the League Championship game against Delaware, their batter with the bases loaded and two outs in the bottom of the sixth had a grand slam homerun after he struck out. You probably would ask how this could happen so here it is. On a drop third strike, our manager thought our catcher had stepped on home plate for the third out, but instead rolled the ball out to the pitcher's mound. Our team ran off the field thinking the inning was over. Meanwhile, the Delaware runners, including the batter, circled the bases for four runs and took the lead. We ended up losing the game.

Memories of Tim: We were standing together at the Sigma Nu fraternity house at Miami University when I pointed across the room at a young lady and told you that she was going to be my future wife; Laurie still is my wife today. I also remember your nasty slider and winning both ends of a double header against Bowling Green.

Work history: 40 years as law partner with Kemp, Schaeffer and Rowe Co. LPA

Biggest Influence: Grandfather Dick Hessey

"Coach of State Champion Worthington High School 2014"

Scouting Report

HE WAS A TRUE SCHOLAR ATHLETE AT MIAMI University, who went on to become a founding partner in his law firm in Columbus, Ohio. Has a true passion for the sport as evidenced not only in his playing style, but also by going on to coach after his playing career ended. A multitasker who was able to successfully blend sports, academics, and a fraternity social life together during his college career. Happy to say after 45 years we have renewed the friendship in Southwest Florida.

Bullpen Session

Baseball Lingo

WHILE EVERY SPORT HAS ITS UNIQUE TERMINOLOGY and language, I don't think any other sport has more unique lingo than baseball. It virtually has a language of its own. If you Google the term Baseball Lingo you'll get an A-Z compilation of terms and sayings accumulated over its hundred plus year history. The letter "B" alone has 102 different entries. No doubt that a lot of the baseball jargon is a result of sports writers or radio and television announcers coining a phrase as they put their own unique spin on the game. I'm sure there is an origin or historical meaning behind each phrase like "Can of corn," "Ducks on the pond," or "A sporting news single." As kids we invented our own little jingles to deride the other team like "Rally Rally Pitchers name is Sally," or telling the pitcher he had "An arm like a leg" or "Stick a fork in him, I think he's done."

Baseball also has its own scoring system to chart the results of the game. Back in the radio days, it wasn't uncommon for people to sit at home and keep a scorebook record of the game. When you went to the ballpark they gave you a program with the team roster and a 9-inning scorecard. That doesn't happen today. My grandfather, a lifelong Chicago Cubs fan, spent many afternoons listening to the Cubs on the radio and keeping score. Every player is numbered by position (1-9) and there are abbreviations for virtually everything that could happen in the game like a sacrifice (Sac), a double (2b), hit by a pitch (hbp), and even a strikeout swinging (K), or looking (a backwards K). You track the runners going around the bases, filling in the diamond if they scored. It's clearly a lost art.

Also in the 50's and 60's, the players seemed to be more glorified than today's players with colorful nicknames like Bambino, The Say Hey Kid, Stan the Man, and Hammerin' Hank. Maybe the reason is our era of political correctness or the fact players' move from team to team in free agency and they never really become a Folk Hero like the players in the past. There are a few exceptions, like Big Papi or Papa Grande, but certainly not like in the Golden Era of baseball 1920-1960. Things were simpler back in the Golden Era. Players would travel by train; the salaries were such that they had to have off season jobs and the rosters tended to be more stable from year to year. We need more personalities back in the game like Charlie Hustle or the Georgia Peach, but I'm afraid free agency, Saber metrics/Analytics, and enormous television revenue have changed the character of the game forever.

Baseball Quote

"Baseball is the only field of endeavor where a man can succeed three out of ten times and be considered a good performer."

- Ted Williams.

SIXTH INNING

IN BETWEEN MY COLLEGE YEARS, I PLAYED SUMMER
baseball. Having graduated from American Legion, it was now necessary
to find an amateur summer league. This wasn't difficult as I was directed
by my Cincinnati scout, Dale McReynolds, to the Skokie Indians, a team
located south of Lake Bluff down the lakefront towards Chicago. The
coach of the team was Bud Blumenthal—an absolute baseball fanatic.
He had a pitching machine and a full batting cage that took up the entire
backyard of his house. This semipro league was comprised of eight teams
stocked with college players, ex minor league ball players, and other life
time amateur lovers of the game.

Having played a limited freshman schedule at college my arm was
reasonably sound and I had an exceptional first season with the Indians.

In one of the final games of the year, leading up to the State Tournament, I pitched against our eventual league winners, the Chicago Saxtons. This was an all African American, south side of Chicago team that played right on Lake Shore Drive just north of the Science and Industry Museum. Today whenever we visit our daughters in Chicago we drive right by the field and I always say to my wife "Do you know I played on that field?" The answer I receive is, "Yes, you tell me every time we drive by."

As a result of a good outing against the Saxtons, they invited me to play with them in the state tournament. They were a great group of guys, very good players, always smiling and laughing, and always teaching me some new baseball lingo. They were very nurturing and would tell me "Kid, I think you're going to make it." It was a great experience.

In the state tournament in Joliet, Illinois, under the lights, we faced the Midlothian White Sox, a powerhouse team from the south side of Chicago. They had a super star pitcher named Johnny Lucenta. He was a gold medal winner in exhibition baseball at the 1968 Mexico City Summer Olympics. He had a lengthy amateur career ultimately pitching in the vintage division of the Roy Hobbs Senior League for guys 65 years and older. I was the starting pitcher for the Saxtons. My father arrived at the game a little late and said, "I looked out on the mound and there you were with seven happy fielders behind you." It was a pitcher's battle that we lost, and eventually the Midlothian team won the state tournament to qualify for the national tournament in Wichita, Kansas. Midlothian invited me to play with them in the National tournament. While this was an exciting honor, by now my arm was starting to tire, and while pitching in Wichita , I knew I was headed for trouble. With no time to rest after the tournament, I headed right to college for fall tryouts for the Varsity at Miami. This boy's baseball career had probably peaked at this point. In fact, after sophomore and junior year at Miami University, I didn't play summer baseball in order to give my arm a much-needed rest.

Lesson Learned

SUMMER BASEBALL DURING MY COLLEGE YEARS added a different dynamic to the game. I was playing with teammates in their 30's and 40's. Many of them were former professional players still competing for the love of the game. They were a tremendous source of knowledge and inspiration. Many had tried to make it at the professional level and failed but continued to play and cherished being on the diamond. They were nurturing and encouraging towards me and it made me feel that maybe I could accomplish what they were not able to do. At times I felt that they were vicariously living their journey of making it to the "show" through me. They demonstrated to me that you could give back to the game, and that your "voice of experience" can provide valuable guidance and help others develop their skill set. It showed me that you played the game because you loved it, regardless of the level of success you achieved.

On the Roster

"Bud and Dick Jirsa on the occasion of his 200th victory at Miami University"

Name: Forrest Middaugh

Nickname: Bud

Hometown: Chambersburg, PA

Height: 6'2"

Weight: 175 pounds

Career: Played two years of football at Miami University and four years of baseball for Coach Woody Wills

Bats: Right

Throws: Right

Positions played: Shortstop, pitcher, and first baseman

Current Residence: Fort Lauderdale, Florida

First Baseball Memory: Listening to the Dodgers/Giants game on the radio in 1951 when Bobby Thompson hit the "shot heard round the world" off of Ralph Branca.

First baseball glove: Used catcher's mitt

Favorite team: Pittsburgh Pirates

Favorite Player: Ralph Kiner-Pittsburgh Pirates

Baseball History: Miami Sports Hall of Fame inductee in 1981 and Cradle of Coaches inductee in 2016. Head Baseball coach at Miami University 1968-1979. Head Baseball coach at University of Michigan 1980-1989. Overall coaching record in college 824-319-1. Players to make it to the majors include Buddy Schultz, Billy Doran, Jack Kucek, Barry Larkin, Chris Sabo, Mike Matheny, Hal Morris, and Jim Abbott.

Unique Baseball Experience: I remember when the University of Michigan played at Miami University and traveling from the hotel to the stadium we stopped by a corn field to warm up for game. My coaching philosophy was "If you do your job as a coach, your team will do well." Recruit well and play together.

Memory of Tim: A lot of ability, but frustrated with constant arm trouble.

Work History: Head baseball coach in High School and college

Biggest influence: Work ethic of my father and the sacrifice he made for me to play baseball at 4 different High Schools

"Bud at "Cradle of Coaches" Induction Ceremony

Scouting Report

PERHAPS THERE WAS NO BETTER FUNDAMENTALS coach in America during his era than Bud Middaugh. He was tough, intense, and driven to succeed. He was a great recruiter, teacher, and helped many of his players achieve their goal of playing at the Major League level. He was demanding of his players and uncompromising with his discipline. Highly competitive, whether it was on the handball court or the baseball diamond. I saw him scuffle with opposing coaches, chase umpires off the field, and take tough disciplinary action with senior class players. The result was that he became a Cradle of Coaches Inductee, Miami Sports Hall of Fame member, and had an impressive career winning percentage.

On the Roster

"Dick in his own "Field of Dreams" Wadsworth, Ohio 2018'

Name: Dick Jirsa

Nickname: Jirs

Hometown: Oak Park, Illinois

Height: 5"9'

Weight: 175 pounds

Bat: Left

Throw: Left

Positions played: Right and center field

Current residence: Wadsworth, Ohio

First baseball memory: Watching the White Sox with Nellie Fox, Billy Pierce, Minnie Minoso, and Jungle Jim Rivera. Catching a foul ball hit by Chico Carrasquel at a White Sox/ Yankee double header

First Glove: Wilson Mickey Mantle model

Favorite Team: Chicago White Sox but now the Cleveland Indians

Favorite Player: Nellie Fox-Chicago White Sox

Baseball History: Winning the Pony League World Series in 1960 and making the Miami University team as a walk-on and starting my junior year. Meeting Bud Middaugh my first week of graduate school and becoming an assistant baseball coach. This changed my life forever.

Best baseball memory: Coaching my son Casey (yes, Casey) from age 8-18 and watching him hit a grand slam over the center field fence at Cooper Stadium in Columbus, Ohio to win the state title for Tallmadge, Ohio. He went on to become a first team all American and ESPN academic all American at Ashland University. Casey promised his critically ill grandfather that he would hit a homer for him the next day and then hit three homeruns on three pitches. Watching 50 former Miami players come back 40 years later to honor Bud Middaugh for his induction into Miami University "Cradle of Coaches."

Unique Baseball Experience: Dick built his own "Field of Dreams" full sized baseball diamond on his property in Ohio. There he hosted numerous amateur tournaments and is currently reconfiguring his field to Little League standards for his grandsons.

Memories of Tim: You threw as hard as anyone and showed us that good ball players can be good students and good people. You were a tough competitor!

Work history: 31 years as an accountant for Smuckers last 28 years as controller.

Biggest Influence: Dick Haley, my Little League coach and Jack Kaiser, my coach at Oak Park High School. Also playing catch with my father as a young boy.

"Dick and Bud at Induction ceremony weekend"

Scouting Report

DICK IS ONE OF MY TOP TWO DRAFTEES FOR MY "Baseball Junkie" All Star team. A walk on member with the Miami University team, a graduate Accounting professor, and assistant varsity coach, Dick successfully blended academic achievement with his love for baseball. This has continued throughout his life having had a highly successful career in finance that allowed him to build his own big league baseball diamond. Kevin Costner has nothing on this guy. With a collegiate All American son, Casey, and four grandsons the next generation of baseball prodigies is in the pipeline. Dick gets the Baseball Passion Award and embodies the spirit and essence of my writing endeavor.

P.S. Thanks Dick for helping me through my Accounting Courses at Miami.

Bullpen Session

Superstition

Another facet of sports that I think is particularly prevalent in baseball is superstition. So often you hear about Major League players that don't change their socks if they are on a winning streak or the manager never steps on the 3rd base line when he visits the mound. Of course if a guy has a no-hitter going, he is isolated in the dugout and no one can talk to him or it will jinx the next inning.

Even the fans get in on the action with their favorite jersey or sporting a rally cap in the closing innings if their favorite team is behind. We all know the story of the "Curse of the Bambino" when the Boston Red Sox sold Babe Ruth to the Yankees after he helped them win four World Series. They never won again until 2004 when they broke the curse. Thankfully the Chicago Cubs broke their "Curse of the Billy Goat" by finally winning the World Series in 2016 after a 108-year drought. Go Cubs Go!

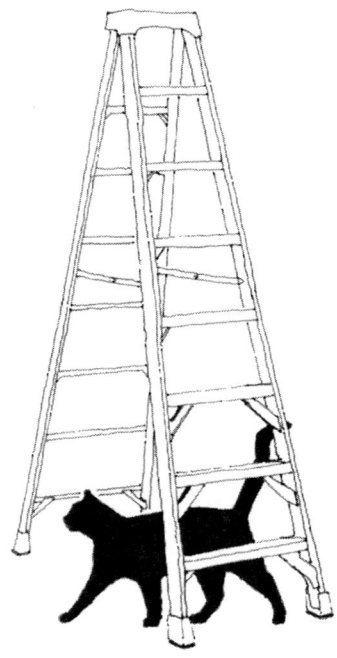

Sometimes what starts out as a simple routine prior to a game becomes an obsessive requirement for fear that if altered only bad things will happen. Players often eat the same pregame meal, warm up the same way before each game, and follow a very specific routine—you don't want to mess with fate. Can you believe that Matt Carpenter of the St. Louis Cardinals attributes their 2018 winning streak to eating his magic salsa before every game? I can be accused of following a similar pattern in how I dressed for the game. Always the same order of putting on the uniform. I'm particularly careful to make sure my sock stirrups have the lower side in the front, pants turned inside out, and the bottom pulled up to just below the knees, carefully turning the socks down over the pants and then pulling the pants up to my waist to complete the ritual. Failure to do it this way for every game could only spell disaster. I can't say I have any statistics to support this assertion, but I am sure it is true and should never be challenged.

Famous Quote

"Baseball is a red blooded sport for red blooded men.
It's no pink tea and Molly Coddlers had better stay out.
It's a struggle for supremacy, survival of the fittest."

- Ty Cobb

NATIONAL	1	2	3	4	5	6	7	8	9	10	R	H	E
CIN	0	1	0	0	0	0	1				2	5	0
CUBS	0	0	1	0	0	1					2	4	0

SEVENTH INNING

WITH COLLEGE GRADUATION AND THE BEGINNING OF my career at Ford Motor Company, for all practical purposes, my hardball career came to an end—but not quite. Because while your body says it's over, your heart isn't quite ready to hang up the spikes. There was still a little gas left in the tank and maybe a little something more to prove.

A Ford transfer back to the Chicago area in 1972 opened up the first postscript of my hardball career, playing for my hometown area team. The Lake Forest Travelers competed in the Shoreline League comprised of communities north, up the lakefront from Chicago. The team had a couple of my old High School teammates and a few LFHS grads currently playing in college.

Having not picked up a baseball for two years, I found myself in uniform and ready to pitch against a familiar rival, Waukegan, Illinois. Since I had not been on the mound for two years, I decided I had to try something a little different. I was worried about trying to snap off a curveball or slider, let alone the challenge of getting the ball over the plate. For the first time in my entire pitching career, I decided I'd try to throw a changeup. Believe it or not I had no idea how to do that; I never really had a pitching coach. Should I alter my grip or change my motion. Warming up before the game I just said to myself, "I just have to preserve my fast ball motion and make the ball take longer to get to the plate." I had a plan, it seemed easy, and surprisingly it worked. I had a no hitter through six innings with my newfound change of speed. Waukegan got a couple hits in the 7th, but we won three-two. I was back in the game. The Waukegan coach was quoted in the paper that week saying "That Boese kid had an excellent fastball and a terrific curveball." Wrong, never threw a curveball just my newly minted changeup. The next morning I could barely get out of bed I was so stiff and sore. I realized how important all of the conditioning work was that we did at Miami University. Bud, you were right, pitchers can't run enough.

I pitched well all summer, had good life on my fastball (yes Tim Love), started throwing a few breaking balls and continued with my new weapon, the changeup. If only I had known how effective changing speeds could have been, perhaps I could have saved my arm and even had a shot, albeit slim, at a professional contract. It was a great summer season back with the boys, playing the game that I love. But that summer was my last official season on the hardball diamond. With work demands and starting a family it was time to hang up the spikes. While I wasn't playing hardball anymore, the love affair was still strong—the passion for the game of baseball will never die

(Ok, before I go on it's time for one of baseball's most endearing traditions, that's right, the seventh inning stretch and time to sing "Take me out to the Ballgame" So stand up, go to the fridge for a beer, and when you are ready Harry Caray will lead us in song…ok, so a "one" and a "two")

It only took 25 years to once again fully ignite the hardball flame. For my 50th birthday my wife presented me with a trip to Detroit Tiger's Fantasy Camp, an annual event in Lakeland, Florida. There you can live out your professional baseball fantasy and play against former big league ball players. In my case, this trip actually resulted in renewing an old friendship with a childhood Little League friend, Mike Maiman.

At Fantasy Camp, the campers are divided into teams and coached by former Tigers, in my case Mickey Lolich, one of the greatest left handed pitcher's of all time, and outfielder Willie Horton. Both were members of the Tigers 1968 World Championship team and two of the greatest Tigers ever. While I've always stayed in pretty good shape, I hadn't thrown a hardball in 25 years. So to prepare for camp, I spent a little time trying to get my legs in shape and even tossed the ball with one of my Ford coworkers inside a Ford Service School Facility.

While that helped some, it didn't prevent baseball instincts from taking over during my first days in Lakeland. I made a quick move for a fly ball in the outfield and I pulled my left hamstring. That's the bad news. The good news was that I sat out the next day and spent two hours sitting on the bench talking with "Mr. Tiger", Al Kaline. With some treatment from the Tiger medical staff, I was still able to pitch and hit with the assistance of a courtesy runner. For a 50-year-old guy, I more than held my own throwing strikes with reasonable velocity and even hitting well (love those aluminum bats). Then in the Fantasy Game, when the campers play against the ex-Tigers, Mickey Lolich tried to slip a knuckle curve by me, I almost took him "yard" (baseball lingo for a home run). I hit the ball to the base of the left center field wall, (370 feet from home plate) the longest ball hit in the game, by either team. The ex-Tigers were yelling "show off" at me from their dugout as I limped to first base. It was music to my ears.

My final brush with hardball occurred when I had the honor of throwing out the first pitch at a Miami University baseball game. Ironically it was against Bowling Green, my career highlight when I won both ends of the double header. My wife and daughters from Chicago, Caroline and Meredith (we're all Miami University grads) surprised me when I went to the mound, by holding up a sign behind home plate. The sign said "Gas $20, Lunch at Mac and Joe's $50, dad throwing out the first pitch, priceless." What a thrill for me. After I threw the pitch, the entire Miami team came out to the mound and presented me with an autographed baseball to thank me for my support of the baseball program. I told them to enjoy their years at Miami; it will be the best time of your life.

Lesson Learned

MY FINAL BRIEF STINT WITH HARDBALL AFTER COL-
lege was very gratifying. It made me appreciate that I had a God-given talent that allowed me to experience some wonderful opportunities. I got to
play with and meet outstanding people that had helped shape me as a person. I had coaches at all levels, including my father, that dedicated them-
selves to not only help players achieve their optimum potential but also to
develop the skills and talents necessary to succeed in life after baseball.

I gained valuable lessons in teamwork and understood the need to
be prepared in order to achieve a desired outcome. There is no question
in my mind that the skills and lessons learned from baseball helped to
guide my business career with Ford Motor Company and my personal
relationships. The leadership and mentoring skills that I learned from
my coaches were instrumental in my success with Ford and as a Lincoln
Mercury Auto dealer. Team building, collaboration, creating a common
vision, and striving for a desired outcome occur on the diamond as well

as in the boardroom. Baseball diamonds, basketball courts, and football fields are every bit as important a place to learn as a High School or college classroom.

On the Roster

"Mike with his Lake Bluff Little League cap 1958"

Name: Mike Maiman

Nickname: Stickman

Hometown: All over the country—father was a Captain in the Navy

Height: 6'0"

Weight: 165 pounds

Bats: right

Throw: right

Positions played: Centerfield in college

Current Residence: Beverly Hills, Michigan

First baseball memory: Walking out of the tunnel at Wrigley Field and seeing the bright green grass. I also loved watching Mark "the Bird" Fidrych when he pitched for the Tigers and sadly attending his funeral in 2009. Favorite team: 1984 Detroit Tigers

Favorite player: Alan Trammell - Detroit Tigers, but I would have loved to have met Ty Cobb.

Baseball History: Was fifth in nation in stolen bases my junior year of college. Earned 10 Varsity letters in football, baseball, basketball and track at Lake Forest College. I was inducted into their Sports Hall of Fame.

Unique Baseball Experience: 15 years attending Tiger Fantasy Camp and got to throw out the first pitch at a Detroit Tigers game. Witnessed Nolan Ryan and Randy Johnson's 300th wins. Having an extensive sports memorabilia collection of one-of- a-kind items.

Memories of Tim: Our fathers' coached Little League baseball together in Lake Bluff, Illinois. You were a great pitcher even then, and we reconnected at Tiger Fantasy Camp.

Work History: Began career with IBM, but formed my own highly successful computer leasing company.

Biggest Influence: Ernie Banks - Chicago Cubs was my inspiration.

"Mike and big brother Dick"

Scouting Report

HE WAS A TRUE SCRAPPER ON THE BASEBALL FIELD
and terrific all around athlete having earned 10 varsity letters in college.
The consummate team player that is as competitive and driven to win today
as he was 60 years ago in the Lake Bluff Little League. He is also a Detroit
Tiger's Fantasy Camp regular and an avid sports memorabilia collector.
Mike would definitely be a member of my most unique characters All Star
team, particularly if loyalty is a priority for your team, then Mike would
be the captain. If you are his friend, you are a friend for life. After playing
together in Little League 60 years ago we now live less than a mile apart.

On the Roster

"Steve coaching the Tigers at Spring Training 2008"

Name: Steve Nagengast

Nickname: Nags

Hometown: Fort Knox, KN

Height: 6"1'

Weight: 180 pounds

Bats: Right

Throws: Right

Current Residence: West Muskegon, Michigan

First baseball memory: Wearing my first Little League uniform while living in New Jersey, I was playing for the Sunny's Sunoco Yankees.

First glove: Mickey Mantle model

Favorite Team: Detroit Tigers

Favorite Player: Rocky Colavito, he was with the Cleveland Indians but was traded to the Tigers with Harvey Keane

Baseball highlight: In the Tigers fantasy camp I was bowled pulled over at home plate, just like Pete Rose did to Ray Fosse in the 1970 All Star game. I did not drop the ball, but had to go to the hospital for x-rays.

Unique Experience: At a charity auction I won the opportunity to co-manage the Tigers with Jim Leyland in a spring training game. I also collect autograph Detroit Tiger baseballs. I currently have almost 1000 individually signed baseballs in my collection, no doubt the largest collection in the world. Needless to say, I am a loyal Detroit Tiger fan.

Memories of Tim: I remember playing with you at Tiger Fantasy Camp; you were the best player on the team even with a pulled hamstring.

Work History: Initially worked for IBM then 27 years as a partner in a CPA consulting firm. For the last 10 years, owned two companies that did metal cutting and logistics.

Biggest influence: Russ Thomas my first Little League coach

"Steve and his hero "Mr. Tiger' Al Kaline"

Scouting Report

STEVE IS ONE OF MY OTHER TOP CHOICES FOR MY "Baseball Junkie" All-Star team. Proves you don't have to have a stellar playing career to be passionate about the game of baseball. Perhaps America's #1 Detroit Tiger fan who is willing to go to extremes to demonstrate his devotion to the team. Super guy, successful in business and no doubt will have the old English "D" on his tombstone.

On the Roster

"Rick in front of Price Insurance Lake Forest, Illinois 2018"

Name: Rick Price

Hometown: Lake Forest, Illinois

Height: 6'2"

Weight: 175 pounds

Bats: right

Throws right

Positions played: Outfield and pitcher

Current Residence: Lake Forest, Illinois

First Baseball memory: Itchy wool uniforms provided by the Lake Forest recreation department

First Glove: A 2000 fielding glove, but also had a sweet Wilson catcher's mitt.

Favorite team: Chicago Cubs

Favorite player: Ernie Banks-Chicago Cubs

Baseball History: All Northwest Suburban conference as Junior and Senior. Had a tryout with Atlanta Braves.

Best baseball memory: While playing for the Shoreline Semipro team, the Travelers, I was brought into the game in relief against North Chicago and pitched nine innings and won the game. All my teammates signed the baseball that I still have today

Remembering Tim: I remember Tim as the guy who always drove a brand new Ford.

Work History: President of Price Family Insurance in Lake Forest, Illinois since the age of twenty-one.

Biggest Influence: Bill Amaden, son of Bob a professor at Lake Forest College. Every year he would borrow my mother's station wagon and take a group of boys to a White Sox game.

Scouting Report

YOU HAVE TO ADMIRE A GUY WHO HAD TO DROP OUT of college to take over the family insurance business due to the sudden death of his father. And, more than 40 years later, the business is still going strong. He is an outstanding all around athlete, outgoing and gregarious, and a business leader in my hometown area. Rick is another example of the successful transfer of baseball skills to other sports as he is a terrific golfer.

Bullpen Session

Fantasy Camp

GOING TO FANTASY CAMP WAS A BUCKET LIST ITEM
for me. There are people there from all walks of life, all ages, and a wide
range of playing ability. There is one common denominator; they are all
intensely passionate about baseball. For six days you are immersed in the
baseball culture. You dress in the Tigers spring training locker room, you
practice and play on their fields, you have your meals together, and listen
to Tiger greats like their legendary announcer Ernie Harwell and

"Mr. Tiger" Al Kaline. It all culminates in playing the fantasy game in Joker-Marchant Stadium against the former Tigers. Every fantasy camp attendee gets to hit once and play the field for at least one inning, for a pitcher you get to pitch to a couple hitters. In my case catcher Bill Freehan, who played 15 years for the Tigers and was a five-time Golden Glove winner, and pitcher Dave Rozema, who had a nine-year Big League career. It's surreal and fortunately my parents were able to attend. My friend Mike Maiman, who I reconnected with at camp, has attended 15 times. That is really refusing to give up the dream.

Baseball Quote

"Baseball is 90% mental and the other half is physical"

- Yogi Berra

EIGHTH INNING

WHILE MY HARDBALL CAREER HAD COME TO THE END, my competitive spirit lived on. As many guys do after their bodies can't handle the rigors of playing hardball, I gave up the 9.25" circumference hardball for the 12" softball. So what's really different? You're playing a team sport, the rules are basically the same, and you've got a glove on your hand. It's just older guys playing at a slower speed. Ten men playing in the field and shorter distance to the bases, helped offset father time's effect on your skill set. You still have a round ball and a round bat and you have to hit the ball square. It's just not coming at you at 90 mph. Now you hit a softball lobbed under hand to the plate. But it's a competitive team sport and the camaraderie and community spirit during and after the game is still exceptional.

Slow pitch softball became my avenue for satisfying my desire to continue playing a team sport. Starting with the Longballers in Hanover Park, Illinois to being the token Presbyterian on the St. Mary's softball team in Hudson, Ohio to teams in Memphis and Detroit. I managed to spend the next 30 years (not necessarily every year) on the softball field with the primary goal of having fun and not getting hurt. Fortunately I accomplished both goals.

As Ford Motor Company transfers and family demands squeezed my schedule; I thought it was time to finally give it up (for a while). I did for several years until I retired and we began spending our winters in Naples, Florida. In Florida, I discovered a whole new world of Senior Softball. In Florida, middle-aged and retired guys who had never lost the desire to play the game populated the leagues. So once again, I dragged myself out of retirement, bought a new pair of cleats, oiled up the glove, and threw my aging body onto the field of battle. With a quick call to the Naples Park District, I obtained the name of the commissioner, found out where they played, suited up and headed to the ballpark. I was told they played at nine o'clock so the next night I arrived at the park at 8:30, and saw the field jammed with very young looking teams. I asked one of the players where the old guys played at nine o'clock. He looked at me like I was a demented old man and said, "That's true they play at nine o'clock accept its nine am not nine pm." Welcome to the land of the retired where as the saying goes, "You get up the morning with nothing to do, and at the end of the day you haven't gotten it done."

Now senior softball, usually 50 and older, has a few unique rules to accommodate the aging process. With courtesy runners, no sliding, and a safety base at first to prevent collisions, the goal is to minimize injuries. Quite frankly having enough healthy bodies to play the game is often the biggest challenge. But its value to the human spirit and the joy it brought to the players was unparalleled.

One of the guys on the Naples team they called "The Bird." He was 92 years old, just a little over the age cut off. He was written up in the Naples newspaper with the headline "Softball Saved my Life." If you knew him and played with him, you would know the headline is spot on. He was inspiring. He stopped the ball in the outfield with his foot and someone had to run over to him so he could flip them the ball to get it back into the infield. He used a courtesy runner, but surprisingly was a very effective hitter. It was a joy to have him on the team. Don't get me wrong, we still wanted to win, but a lot of our gratification was just getting to play.

A lot of the guys on the team were from New York and New Jersey and it seemed like half of them were named Sal. It was great group of guys; it got you up and going in the morning. But after a couple years playing in Florida, I decided my golf game took priority.

My final stop on the senior softball circuit occurred back home in the summers in Birmingham, Michigan playing for a local bar, Dick O' Dows. Once again this was a wonderful group of guys who just loved the game, led by our 85-year-old pitcher—Oz Forrester. This was a 50+ league so we had some relatively young guys on the team. My first year, we had a mediocre year and lost in the season ending league tournament. But our hopes were high for the second year as we entered the tournament. Just before the first game, Oz declared he was planning on retiring. The ultimate locker room motivation speech was "win one for the Oz." It was a double elimination tournament and in the first two days, we won our first game but lost our second putting us into the loser's bracket. Going into the third day we would have to win our first game and then beat the remaining undefeated team twice to win the championship. Sue and I were planning on leaving on a driving trip to Montreal and Lake Placid first thing that morning when I explained that we were in an elimination tournament. If we lost, we were out, but if we kept winning we would play three games that day. When she asked me to skip the potential second game, I explained to her that you just don't abandon your team. I was not a popular guy on the home front at that point. Well of course we won the first game to reach the finals, beat the undefeated team in the first game, to set up the winner take all championship game.

Leading 10-2 early we saw our lead whittled away until suddenly it was 10-9 in the bottom of the 7th. Our opponents had the bases loaded with only one out. I was playing first base with a left hand hitter at the plate. One thing about baseball, whether it's hardball or softball, it is a game of anticipation in contrast to football and basketball that are games of reaction. When you're in the field, you have to think about all the different scenarios that could happen and anticipate how you will react if you are involved in the play. In this case, my first thought was that if there was a ground ball to first I'll step on the base for one out and then throw home to get the runner at the plate. In senior softball you merely have to get the ball to the catcher before the runner crosses a chalk line extended out from home plate. The only complication was I had to be careful with my throw, as 82-year-old Kenny was our catcher at the time. It's nice when a plan comes together. The batter hit a sharp ground ball down the first base line. Thankfully, I fielded the ball cleanly, stepped on the base for the first out, took about three extra steps towards home to make sure I made a good throw home to Kenny and bingo Oz retired a champion. I finally left on vacation only six hours late. While this was probably my last competitive game, my passion for baseball is as strong as ever, but now as a spectator and a critic of every player and manager in major league baseball.

Lesson Learned

IN MY SENIOR SOFTBALL DAYS, WHEN I WAS PLAYING with 80 and 90 year olds, I really got a dose of how passionate people can be about a game. There is no question in my mind that "the Bird" in Naples, Florida would never have made 92 without the game of softball. When you're playing a team sport, the game is important but what happens after the game is equally important. The camaraderie and lively conversation as you debate, argue, and replay the key moments in the game is as important as the game itself. If only our bodies could stay as young as our heart and our spirit.

On the Roster

"Oz throwing another strike"

Name: Arnold Forster

Nickname: Oz

Hometown: Butler City, Ohio

Height: 6'1"

Weight: 170 pounds

Bats: right

Throws: right

Positions played: Pitcher in senior softball

First Glove: Double hand-me-down from my siblings

Favorite Team: Cincinnati, Reds

Favorite Player: Pete Rose-Cincinnati Reds

Baseball History: Started playing softball at the age of 50- 12" slow pitch

Current residence: Birmingham, Michigan

Baseball Memory: Went to see the Cincinnati Reds "Big Red Machine." Pete Rose should be in the Hall of Fame.

Best baseball memory: Winning the Senior League Championship in the last year I played. We had to win three games in one day and I pitched all three.

Remembering Tim: Since I coached the team and you were the best player, I always watched the parking lot hoping to see if you were going to arrive for the game.

Work history: Worked for GM as a manufacturing engineer

Biggest Influence: "Charlie Hustle" Pete Rose was my guy.

"Oz with winning trophy after his final victory 2016"

Scouting Report

IT'S ALWAYS GREAT TO GO OUT ON TOP AND THAT'S exactly what Oz did at the age of 85-winning a League Championship. Still competitive, very proud, pitching the entirety of three games his last day playing. No courtesy runner for this guy. You might say that I retired on Oz's coat tails; I just did it when I was 18 years younger. He's a great guy, an inspiration, and a living example that baseball can be a lifetime sport.

On the Roster

" Jimmy swinging for the fences...again"

Name: Jim Luzod

Nickname: Chico

Hometown: Pontiac, Michigan

Height: 5'6"

Weight: 130 pounds

Bats: right

Throws: right

Positions played: Utility player

Current hometown: Bloomfield Hills, Michigan

First baseball memory: In grade school went to two elementary schools and went home crying because they wouldn't let me play because I had just transferred to the school. My next year, 5th grade, I joined the team.

First glove: Rawlings G600 - Marty Marion Edition

Favorite team: Detroit Tigers

Favorite player: Al Kaline-Detroit Tigers

Baseball history: Played in recreational Little League in Pontiac. Started playing softball at 22 and I'm still playing at 74. For 13 years I have gone to the World Series of softball in Utah. I've played through rotator cuff problems, meniscus tears in both knees, and stem cell injections.

Baseball memories: At Central Michigan University, I tried out for the JV team, got to bat against their best pitcher, Fred Geise, who hit me in the back of the leg—it was a red badge of honor.

Unique Baseball Experience: Playing a game in Redford, Michigan I was the cutoff man at second base and I relayed the throw home and the catcher tagged out two guys trying to score.

Remembering Tim: First time I saw you swing a bat, I thought if I could swing a bat like that I would've played in college.

Work history: Taught physical education for 4 1/2 years at Farmington Hills High School then became a State Farm Agent for 27 years

---

Biggest influence: My step-father (Don Johnson). At eight years old we played catch in a parking lot

---

"Jimmy hitting behind the runner...finally"

Scouting Report

JIM IS THE POSTER BOY FOR SENIOR SOFTBALL. THE poster says "I will play the game until the day that I physically can't walk onto the field." Through knee injuries, bruises, aneurysms, Jimmy keeps playing. It's a joy to watch him play, constantly chattering, and moving around on the field, coaching and encouraging his teammates, and trying to inspire his team. He is highly competitive, to the point of still getting tossed out of games. Jim's enthusiasm is contagious and I hope it can go on for many years.

On the Roster

"Joe 2018"

Name: Joe Chavara

Nickname: Stretch

Hometown: Farrell, PA

Height 6'1"

Weight 180

Bats: right

Throws: right

Position played; First base

Current residence Palm Coast, Florida

First baseball memory: Played Little League baseball and I was really better at defense than offense, even though my last year I was the homerun leader with two.

Favorite team: Pittsburgh Pirates

Favorite Player: Roberto Clemente-Pittsburgh Pirates

Baseball History: Played Little League baseball through Babe Ruth league in Ferrell, Pennsylvania. Tried out at West Point for baseball, but didn't make the team.

Unique baseball experience: After leaving the army, I went to work for Ford Motor Company in Chicago (Tim was my first boss). I was invited to join a 16" softball team and when I showed up with my glove everyone started laughing. I realized you don't use gloves with 16" softball.

Baseball memory: Playing softball with the Longballers in Chicago, my wife Barbara was four weeks overdue the night of one of our games. Just as we were headed to the game her water broke. I talked Barb into going to the game since it was on the way to the hospital. Not a popular decision with all the wives at the game.

Remembering Tim: When I played with the Longballers, I was usually the catcher and Tim played left center. On one particular play with a runner on first the hitter drove the ball over the left fielder's head. Tim raced back got the ball and unleashed what became known as "the throw." On the line from deep left field to home, a wild collision with the runner left me lying across home plate holding onto the ball. The "throw" didn't get the batter out at home; it got the runner at first base out at home, on a play where both the runner and batter should have easily scored.

Work history: Worked for Ford Motor Company from 1978-1994 and then became a Ford & Lincoln Mercury dealer in multiple locations in Florida

Biggest Influence: My father, Bill, was coach of the Corpo-Russ team and I was the batboy.

"Joe throwing out first pitch at Tampa Bay Rays game"

Scouting Report

PERHAPS THERE IS NO PERSON THAT I HAVE EVER MET in my life with more character than Joe Chavara. Joe is the oldest sibling of eleven, who lost his father at a young age. A West Point Grad who I hired to work at Ford Motor Company. Perhaps my best draft choice ever. Joe elected to leave Ford Motor Company and became a highly successful Ford and Lincoln Mercury dealer in multiple locations in Florida. Outstanding teammate, coworker, and friend.

On the Roster

" Rick with his corporate look"

Name: Eric Graves

Nickname: Rick

Hometown: Groton, New York

Height: 5'9"

Weight: 155 pounds

Bats: Right

Throws: Right

Current residence: Cumming, GA

Positions played: Second base in high school

First baseball memory: Being a huge Yankees fan at five-years-old and starting Little League at age eight.

First glove: Wilson A2000

Favorite team: New York Yankees

Favorite player: Bobby Richardson-New York Yankees

Baseball History: Hit .365 my senior year and was MVP of Groton HS team

Baseball memories: Going to Doubleday field in Cooperstown, New York in August 1959 and getting Ty Cobb's autograph. Our family had a cottage on Otsego Lake in Cooperstown and Bobby Richardson was our neighbor.

Unique Baseball Experience: I have an autographed baseball of the entire Yankees '61, '62, and '63 teams. My brother Terry was two for three off of Ralph Terry (11 years in the majors) in an All Star game against the Yankees rookies.

Memories of Tim: As Tim's college roommate and fraternity brother at Miami University, I went to many of his baseball games and I'm glad I didn't have to face his fastball. Tim and I played for many years together with the Longballers. While he was a good hitter, it was his arm that was most memorable—gunning down many naive runners who never thought a guy that deep had a chance of getting them out. Tim also never let his emotions affect his athletic goals. As a result he was able to keep his eye on the target of winning

Work History: Spent 44 years in the Travel Industry retiring as Vice President of Sales for Crystal Cruises.

Biggest Influence: Brother Terry Graves—but also Jim Konstanty—National League MVP in 1950

"Rick and Tim at Parent's Weekend in Oxford, Ohio 2001"

Scouting Report

TENACIOUS, COMPETITIVE, AND WILLING TO GET DIRTY.
He is a fierce competitor at any sport. Sweats more than any athlete whom
I've ever known. Roommates in college, roommates after college, we mar-
ried Chicago roommates who went to Miami, and all of our kids went to
Miami University. It's quite obvious a lifetime of friendship and respect.
We've been through wonderful time's together and challenging times but
that's what friends are for. Have attended annual fraternity brother golf
outing together for 45 straight years and still going strong.

On the Roster

" Steve in is Longballers jersey Hanover Park,Illinois 1973"

Name: Steve Williams

Nickname: Willy

Hometown: Arlington Heights, Illinois

Height: 6'1"

Weight: 180 pounds

Bats: Right

Throws: Right

Positions played: Pitcher

Current residence: St. Johns, Florida

First Baseball Memory: Started playing baseball at eight years old in Rockford, IL recreational summer league.

First glove: Spaulding

Favorite team: 1959 White Sox. The Chicago Cubs fans were snobs

Favorite player: Hank Aaron-Milwaukee Braves

Baseball History: When I was 16 years old, I was 9-0 and we won the Arlington Heights Pony League. I pitched the first game of a two game playoff then pitched a complete game against the All Star team and won 9-6.

Baseball Highlight: Pitched against Dave Kingman in High School who played in the big leagues for 15 years and hit 442 homeruns. I also played on 1985 Longballers softball team, which qualified for national tournament. We beat Kentucky and Minnesota teams and finished 11th out of 132 teams.

Memories of Tim: He batted 3rd or 4th in line up as one of our power hitters, but saved my bacon many times in left field catching balls hit over his head and throwing runners out trying to take an extra base.

Work History: Worked in Forest Product Industry for my entire career

Biggest influence: My father Wally was always willing to play catch with me. He was a big baseball fan. Also Mr. Donohue, who played for the Phillies, taught me how to pitch.

"Finishing another Triathlon- Panama City, Florida 2014"

Scouting Report

CONSTANT, STEADY, AND SOLID IS PROBABLY THE WAY to describe Steve. He is an All American boy who is a quiet leader on the field. This was the beginning of my softball era and you quickly discovered whether it was hardball or softball it was the teammates like Steve that made it special. He is the type of guy who holds a team together by always nurturing and encouraging his team, and never giving up until the final out. While Steve has retired from softball, he satisfies his competitive desire, quite successfully, by competing in Triathlons.

Bullpen Session

Statistics

BASEBALL IS A GAME OF VOLUMINOUS STATISTICS. Virtually every aspect or potential outcome of the game is measured, calculated, and tabulated. One of the biggest changes in the game is compiling mountains of statistics and actually utilizing the data to make game time decisions and to evaluate players and prospects. The Oakland Athletics, under GM Billy Beane essentially popularized the term Saber metrics glorified in the book and movie "Moneyball." You can collect and analyze baseball statistics and use the results to determine the probability of success of draft choices and the probability of potential outcomes in game time decisions.

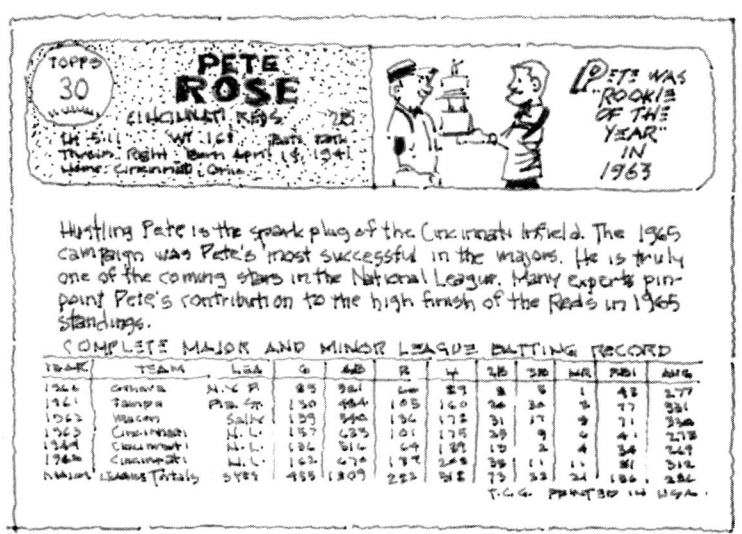

Today's teams are literally establishing an Analytics Department in their organization. The managers and coaches may even have a laptop or I Pad in the dugout. Literally everything that can occur in a baseball game is quantified. The acronyms are endless WAR, OPS, WHIP, let alone ERA and BA. Managers have access to data not only on each opposing batter against each pitcher, but also by pitch type, by pitch count, and by quadrant of the strike zone. It's hard to believe that Sparky Anderson or Casey Stengel would have had the patience or even the aptitude to analyze and utilize the data available today. But Big Money drives big changes and pushes organizations to search for anything that may give them a competitive advantage. Unfortunately the level of analytics has slowed down the pace of the game and turned managers into statisticians instead of tacticians.

Baseball Quote

"Baseball was, is, and always will be, to me, the best game in the world"

- Babe Ruth.

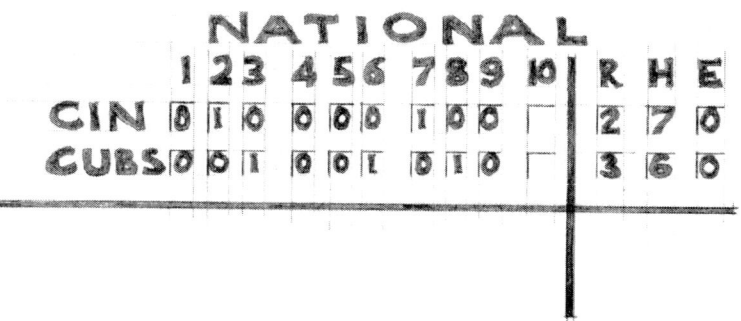

NATIONAL	1	2	3	4	5	6	7	8	9	10	R	H	E
CIN	0	1	0	0	0	0	1	0	0		2	7	0
CUBS	0	0	1	0	0	1	0	1	0		3	6	0

NINTH INNING

WHILE I'D LOVE TO THINK MY LITERARY JOURNEY
would go into extra innings, it won't, but alas it didn't end with the mercy
rule. I would like to think there was something I could have done differ-
ently, like having thrown fewer curve balls or had a surgical procedure,
but the probability was I was not built to last. I have no regrets, I gave it
my best and had years of personal satisfaction and success with the game.
Life goes on.

While fundamentally the game of baseball has remained unchanged
over 100 years, the overall culture of baseball is quite different. First and
most obvious is the magnitude of the game as a business. Television contracts have exploded the revenue pool and player contracts, largely driven
by free agency, have skyrocketed. In 1947 Hank Greenberg was the first

to make $100,000 annually, and 32 years later in 1979 Nolan Ryan was the first $1 million dollar a year ball player. This year when Bryce Harper hits free agency, his agent's goal is a $400 million dollar contract over 10 years. The minimum major league salary has grown from $21,000 in 1978 to $535,000 in 2017 but the average salary is $4.38 million. Most rosters even have several players making millions of dollars per year that are hitting below the Mendoza line. In 1979 this was defined as a 200 batting average or less and was considered unacceptable for a major league player.

While I know these elite athletes have made the "Show," one would think with the incredible salaries today players should be able to afford a haircut and razor blades. I give the New York Yankees and George Steinbrenner props for their personal grooming requirements for their players. I think it sets a better example for the youth of America. The demographics in baseball have also changed dramatically. Currently, almost 30% of major league players are from Latin America. The percentage of African American players has dropped into single digits perhaps driven by an often single parent household, prioritizing other sports, and lack of a formal Little League organizations and diamonds in urban areas. Fortunately, I think there are positive initiatives in play to improve African American participation levels.

Baseball has become more of a world sport. There is a greater interchange between the US and Japan and players from 18 different countries are currently represented in the major leagues. No position on the roster has undergone more adaptation and change than the pitcher. From the days when the starting pitcher took the mound every 4th game with no limit to his pitch count now starters usually pitch every fifth day. There are middle relievers, set up men, and closers. And of course the American League has designated hitters. Oh for the days of Mickey Lolich who won three complete games in the 1968 World Series in the span of eight days, clearly no pitch count was in effect for Mickey.

The evolution of the variety of pitches thrown is also remarkable. In the 1970s, the primary pitches were the fastball, curveball, and changeup. There were specialty pitches like the forkball and knuckleball. Now pitchers repertoire could include a cut fastball, two and four seam fastballs, circle changes, and multiple grips on the ball. Pitching has truly become a science.

Excluding professional baseball, aluminum bats have altered the game. The bats are lighter, easier to swing, and allow the hitter to turn inside or outside pitches into hits. I am glad I wasn't pitching from 60 ft. 6 inches to guys with aluminum bats. They add an additional element of danger for the pitcher. Growing up with wooden bats also added an element of character and sensuality to the game. You might use the Nellie Fox model bottle bat or the thin handled Rocky Colavito bat. Now it's just the Mizuno and Eaton model and they certainly are not flame tempered or covered with pine tar. I think there are a lot of guys whose big league careers faltered when they had to switch from aluminum bats used in college or amateur baseball to wooden bats in the professional league.

PEDs and steroids have clearly been a dark cloud over baseball. But I also believe today's players are bigger, stronger, and faster without the help of any supplements. They play 162 games and maybe an extended playoff schedule and face pitchers throughout a 9-inning game throwing 95-100 mph fastballs. There overall conditioning is better than the Golden Era Players, but of course this is their year round profession versus when players actually had off-season jobs to supplement their income. The game has changed and baseball competes with so many other choices of entertainment.

There are many other role models, both good and bad, which kids choose to emulate in today's society. The simple desire to hang your glove on the handlebars of your bike and ride to the park in hopes of getting into a pickup game has been overtaken by the electronic age. My guess is there are fewer sand lot fields in America today. Unfortunately, there are a fewer fathers playing catch with their sons and fewer kids collecting and trading baseball cards. Too bad. These were simple and wholesome activities.

Baseball is really an every man's game, a sport for all sizes. You don't have to be seven-feet tall or weigh 350 pounds to compete in this sport. I've debated many an hour with friends, that baseball players are the best all around athletes. Baseball does not have a ball sitting on the tee; they haven't made the racket bigger or the shaft out of titanium. You run, you jump, you throw, you try to hit a moving target, and you have to think, anticipate, and react at every position you play. What other sport demands such a vast skill set. I still dream at night about my love for the game and hoping I will get called up to "The Show."

Bullpen Session

My Epilogue

EVEN THOUGH I AM NOT PLAYING, MY PASSION FOR the game will never be extinguished. Baseball is a part of the fabric of America. There is no better family activity than a sunny day or a cool summer evening at the ballpark. A hot dog, some peanuts and popcorn, a cold beverage, the green grass, the crack of the bat, and cheering for your favorite player and team; it's perfect. My personal journey in the sport was one of tremendous gratification and joy coupled with physical challenges that ultimately ended my dream.

I have loved this game from my very first memories, playing catch with my brother Tom and having my father coach me for so many years is truly a special way to grow up. I've referenced the movie "Field of Dreams" on several occasions, but can't help utilizing one of its scenes that truly captures my passion and relationship with the game of baseball. In the movie, when Ray Kinsella (Kevin Costner) asks Archie "Moonlight" Graham (Burt Lancaster) if he could grant him one wish what would it be? Archie answers "To bat one time in the big leagues." Ray responds, he could make the dream come true. That it would be a tragedy if he didn't seize the opportunity. Archie replies that it will have to stay a wish. But what would really have been a tragedy is if I only got to be a doctor for five minutes. Many times I have wished and dreamed about playing in the big leagues, but like Doc Graham, I wouldn't have wished or traded it for the path my life has followed. While baseball is my passion, it is still only in the top five behind my family, friends, and faith.

Famous Quote

"This field, this game is a part of our past.

It reminds us of all that was once good and could be again.

People will come."

- Terrance Mann, Field of Dreams

"Miami University 1971"

About the Writer

Name: Timothy Boese

Nickname: Bubba

Hometown: Lake Bluff, Illinois

Height: 6'2"

Weight: 210 pounds

Bats: Right

Throws: Right

Positions Played: Pitcher, catcher, outfield

Current Residence: Beverly Hills, Michigan

First Glove: Richie Ashburn model

Favorite Team: 1959 White Sox

Favorite Player: Orestes "Minnie" Minoso-Chicago White Sox

First baseball memory: Getting hit on the head by a baseball bat by my brother Tom. It was a rough start to my career.

Career highlights: All Conference in High School, All Academic MAC in college, 6 high school years no hitters, one perfect game, drafted by Cincinnati Reds in 1967

Work History: 30 years with Ford Motor Company, nine years as Lincoln Mercury Automotive Dealer

Biggest Influence: My father Harold and brother Tom

"Tim & Tom-only time on same team 1958"

"Colt League Team 1965-Tim back row, third from left"

"Hurling for the Lake Forest Scouts"

"Midlothian White Sox Wichita,Kansas 1968 (Back row third from right)

"Longballers 1983 - (Tim&Sue back row third from right)

"Family Home Lake Bluff"

"Lake Forest High School"

My All Time Favorite Team

First Base: Miguel Cabrera - Detroit Tigers - Perhaps the best right hand hitter ever

---

Second base: Nellie Fox - Chicago White Sox - Second baseman on my favorite team

---

Third Base: Mike Schmidt - Philadelphia Phillies – The only Hall of Famer I pitched against

---

Shortstop: Ernie Banks - Chicago Cubs –"Mr. Cub" - "Let's play Two," need I say more

---

Left Fielder Ken Henderson - Chicago White Sox – Looked great in uniform

---

Right Field: Orestes "Minnie" Minoso - Chicago White Sox –"Mr. White Sox"

Center field: Richie Ashburn - Philadelphia Phillies - my first glove

---

Catcher: Johnny Bench - Cincinnati Reds - Best catcher to play the game

---

Pitcher - Nolan Ryan - Texas Rangers - perfect form, stood the test of time

Manager - Walter "Smokey" Alston - Los Angeles Dodger - Miami University graduate

Owner - Bill Veeck - Chicago White Sox - greatest innovator ever in baseball

Announcer: Ernie Harwell - Detroit Tigers - Long time voice of the Detroit Tigers.

Game summary: Writing "Play Ball" has been a wonderfully enjoyable and fulfilling project. Reconnecting with former teammates and friends, reflecting on the lessons that I've learned, and remembering the moments of triumph and the physical challenges I fought to conquer. Most importantly appreciating the significant role that my father played in my career. My coach, my mentor, and my biggest cheerleader and fan. Thanks to all who were patient with my inquiries and contributed to the finished product. As you can all appreciate it takes a team effort.

Acknowledgements

FIRST AND FOREMOST I WANT TO THANK MY family—my wife, Susan, and daughters, Caroline and Meredith, for their unending support and encouragement for this project. Without them I am lost. To my fellow authors Tim Love, Robert Navarro, and Gerry Haines thank you for your inspiration and guidance. To Terry Demaline, the book's illustrator, what a fabulous job capturing the nostalgic essence of the wonderful game of baseball. To all those who were so patient with me contributing their thoughts and memories for the "On the Roster" profiles—Tom Boese, Brian Lofstrom, Grant Cardinal, Kenny Eiserman, Chuck Johnson, Denny Smith, Tim Love, Steve Rowe, Bud Middaugh, Dick Jirsa, Mike Maiman, Steve Nagengast, Rick Price, Oz Forrester, Jimmy Luzod, Joe Chavara, Rick Graves, and Steve Williams. I value all of you, so much, as teammates, coaches, and most of all, as friends. A special thank you to Bob Shapland, Kaitlin Frohn, and Jill Thomas for their sound advice and artistic counsel. And finally to my father (Harold) and mother (Betty) who so loyally followed my career from diamond to diamond, with my sister Beth in tow, encouraging and nurturing me along my journey.

Profits from this book will be donated to
St. Jude and Shriner's Children Hospitals.